How Do They Know You Care?

THE PRINCIPAL'S CHALLENGE

How Do They Know You Care?

THE PRINCIPAL'S CHALLENGE

Linda L. Lyman

FOREWORD BY ROLAND S. BARTH

Teachers College, Columbia University
New York and London

Published by Teachers College Press, 1234 Amsterdam Avenue, New York, NY 10027

Library of Congress Cataloging-in-Publication Data

Lyman, Linda L.
   How do they know you care? : the principal's challenge / Linda L. Lyman ; foreword by Roland S. Barth.
      p.   cm.
   Includes bibliographical references (p.   ) and index.
   ISBN 0-8077-3930-8 (cloth : alk. paper) — ISBN 0-8077-3929-4 (pbk. : alk. paper)
      1. Principals—Illinois—Case studies.   2. Educational leadership—Illinois—Case studies.
   3. Caring.   4. Hinton, Kenneth H.   I. Title.
   LB2831.924.I3 L96   2000
   371.2'012—dc21   99-058623

ISBN 0-8077-3929-4 (paper)
ISBN 0-8077-3930-8 (cloth)

Printed on acid-free paper
Manufactured in the United States of America

07 06 05 04 03 02 01 00   8 7 6 5 4 3 2 1

Dedicated to my children,
Steve Gale
Elaine Gale
David and Kristine Gale
and my grandson,
Jack Gale

Contents

Foreword

WE HAVE ALL HEARD (and said), "As the principal goes, so goes the school"; "Show me a good school and I'll show you a good principal." A few accounts show us caring principals, but none that I know argues so persuasively and explicitly that a caring principal begets a caring school, and that a caring school is a good school.

Linda Lyman has seen something very special in Kenneth Hinton, principal of the Valeska Hinton Early Childhood Education Center in Peoria, Illinois. Around him she marshals a strong, scholarly, and engaging argument: A caring person can become a caring leader. A caring leader begets caring teachers, parents, students—a caring school community. A caring school environment has a powerful influence upon learning.

I find this finely textured, ethnographic portrait a suitable successor to Harry Wolcott's classic, *The Man in the Principal's Office.* Like Wolcott, Linda Lyman observes the principal for more than two years, and exhaustively describes and analyzes his behavior and influence. But in telling Hinton's story, Lyman, with both ambition and courage, takes on the fuzzy, squishy concept of "caring"—a task akin to "nailing jello to the wall." In the process, she succeeds admirably in bringing clarity, rigor, legitimacy, and immediacy to "caring" in education—all of this in an era where "toughness," "standards," and "testing" currently run roughshod over the educational terrain. No small accomplishment.

Many years ago, when I worked in the admissions office at the Harvard Graduate School of Education, we customarily asked aspiring MAT's, "So why have you chosen a career in education?" Their replies were divided: Some said, "My own schooling was terrific; I want to make sure others have it as good as I." Even more replied, "My school experience was so rotten, I decided to dedicate myself to making sure no other students ever have it so bad." In a curious way, present schools benefit from the destructiveness, as well as the successes, of former schools.

This richly detailed portrait of Ken Hinton reveals an African American youngster abused by life in schools. Resolving that no others will have

it that way, he becomes a caring, nurturing male school administrator—
so unusual in our times, when Joe Clark and his baseball bat get the
recognition.

What *is* caring? How does a principal exercise leadership by caring?
How does a "leader grounded in caring" create a caring culture within an
inner city school? Does it matter, anyway? Is there any relationship between
a caring community and pupil achievement? These are the unusual, fresh,
and refreshing questions Linda Lyman takes on, and, with assistance from
Hinton, addresses.

It might be said of Linda Lyman, as it was said by teachers about Ken
Hinton, that in this volume she has had a lasting, caring influence "by the
way she is and does things." Her "methods can be subtle."

Too many within our profession, a "caring profession," seem to have
lost track of the star of caring. In universities, state departments of education, central offices, schools, and classrooms, preoccupation with "cover-
age," preparation for testing, testing, living with the fallout of testing
prevail. Yet, as this little volume you are about to read suggests, holding
high standards can be caring. Expecting others to meet high standards can
be caring. This is necessary but not sufficient for a school to be good. A
caring culture is one that is humane and hospitable to both life and learning. And that's what schools should be about.

I want to visit Peoria and talk with Ken Hinton, who cares so much
and so well. And I want to visit the Valeska Hinton Education Center, a
caring community. In the meantime, this remarkable, verbal "field trip"
upon which you are about to embark serves all of us quite well indeed.

Roland S. Barth

Preface

AT THE MIDPOINT of my life I earned a doctorate in administration, curriculum, and instruction at the University of Nebraska and made my way to Bradley University in Peoria, Illinois, to learn and teach. I came to Peoria somewhat apprehensively, reserving judgment. To my pleasant surprise, I have found and been taken in by a diverse community of amazing people accomplishing the work of community-building in both common and uncommon ways. This book shares what I have learned about leadership from the privilege of eight years of observing what plays in Peoria. In particular, this book shares a portrait of a principal whose uncommon caring makes a difference. Kenneth H. Hinton is one of Peoria's extraordinary human beings, an educator whose story is not yet finished. His example offers plain and ordinary lessons to ground each of us who hope to reach our full potential as educators and caring persons.

OVERVIEW

In Chapter 1, I introduce a caring principal and school, build a frame to serve as a theoretical context for the portrait, and address the topic of significance. The discussion of significance includes attention to caring's influence on learning, the virtual silence in mainstream educational administration texts about caring as a significant component of school leadership, the nonexistence of practical guides to caring school leadership, and the emergence of universal themes in case study research.

Chapter 2 profiles director/principal Kenneth H. Hinton and the community, neighborhood, and family contexts that have shaped him as a person and an educator. A second section illuminates his career as a calling. Recurring patterns create a silhouette of a principal who is nonconformist, compassionate, and a builder.

Chapter 3 provides a history and comprehensive picture of a family-centered school that is the professional context for Hinton's leadership. The philosophy, organizational structure, and programs for children and their families are described. Best practices of early childhood education are featured, as well as a model parent involvement program. The meaning of the name, Valeska Hinton Early Childhood Education Center, ends the chapter.

Chapter 4 focuses on the school's caring environment. An exploration of the physical environment is followed by results of my 1995–96 research on staff and parents' perceptions of the environment. Perceptions of the school environment reflect the responses of the 61 full-time staff and 40 parents to this interview question: "If you could only use one word to describe the environment of the Valeska Hinton Early Childhood Education Center, what one word would you choose?" The word most frequently chosen (13 of 101) was *caring*. I conclude the chapter by reporting highlights of in-depth interviews with two teachers who have taught in both of the two schools for which Hinton has served as principal.

In the context of contemporary scholarship about the principalship and decision-making, Chapter 5 considers tough decisions Hinton has made. The decisions involved recommending teachers for nonrenewal, stabilizing the program through reconfiguration, and strengthening family involvement by stiffening the consequences for nonparticipation. The conclusion of the chapter depicts Hinton during a typical day, capturing him as an example of caring in his respectful non-role-bound interactions with people, use of time, encouraging manner, problem-solving practices, and commitment to children. Based on observation and school documents as well as focused interviews, the contents of this chapter provide the triangulation necessary to establish the trustworthiness of the six themes of Hinton's leadership developed in the next chapter.

Chapter 6 presents the themes of Hinton's caring leadership that emerged for me through content analysis of the interview data. I have stated the themes as simple descriptive sentences. They are organized by and illustrate Noddings's essential components of caring—engrossment, action, and reciprocity. Two themes capture the engrossment characteristic of Hinton's caring: *His use of time reveals his priorities*, and *he supports and encourages others as persons*. Two themes of his leadership indicate to me that Hinton's caring takes the form of action: *He listens and solves problems*, and *he keeps the mission focused and central*. Finally, at the heart of Hinton is the reality of an underlying attitude of reciprocity, embedded in my final two descriptions of themes of his leadership: *He does not limit himself or anyone else by or to a role*, and *he treats every person equally and with respect*.

In Chapter 7, I turn to the complex question of whether caring leadership enhances learning. Implications of brain research, the Valeska Hinton Center program's learning outcomes, and Hinton's beliefs about the connection between caring and learning are the main topics of the chapter. The argument of the chapter is that caring ought to be a focus of teachers and administrators who would promote the full development of learners, their cognitive as well as their social and emotional learning.

Chapter 8 examines whether the themes of Hinton's leadership at an early childhood center have implications for elementary, middle, and high school principals. Experiences of other principals who have also created caring schools will be reviewed to develop understanding of how caring schools evolve. My analysis identifies leadership practices and challenges typically experienced by principals who work to build more caring environments in their schools.

Chapter 9 develops a leadership metaphor for a new century and explores how one finds a personal path through the complexities and possibilities of school leadership grounded in caring. Caring's layers of complexity include barriers of gender and bureaucracy. Caring's layers of possibility for leadership and school reform include enhancing learning, rebuilding community, and reforging justice.

Throughout the book the actual names of the school, Hinton, faculty, staff, and parents are used with permission. The actual names of children are not used. Each chapter ends with a short list of questions for personal reflection, inspired by the topics covered.

My goal as a writer has been to present an engaging, interpretive, analytical portrait of a caring leader, a portrait of goodness inviting readers not necessarily to emulate, but to reflect. The questions for reflection posed throughout the book offer an opportunity to deepen self-understanding, to become more fully oneself, to find one's own personal path into the future as a caring leader. Sometimes to move forward we must look back, and in so doing sort out, as Dillard's (1974) words suggest, our own complexities and possibilities:

> But there is more to the present than a series of snapshots. We are not merely sensitized film; we have feelings, a memory for information and an eidetic memory for the images of our own pasts. Our layered consciousness is a tiered track for an unmatched assortment of concentrically wound reels. Each one plays out for all of life its dazzle and blur of translucent shadow-pictures; each one hums at every moment its own secret melody in its own unique key. We tune in and out. (p. 84)

ACKNOWLEDGMENTS

I wish to acknowledge the help and support of all those persons who believed in my ability to write this book and helped me accomplish the task.

I am particularly grateful to Ken Hinton, who so generously opened his school to me and shared his energy, time, mind, and life story. Judy Harris Helm and Sandra Burke provided invaluable knowledge and reviewed the draft of Chapter 3. Faculty and staff at the Valeska Hinton Center who shared their time and wisdom included secretaries Jackie Petty and Micheline Pascal; lead teacher Sallee Beneke; classroom teachers Jolyn Blank, Monica Borrowman, Anna Brown, Colleen Brown, Rachel Bystry, Judy Cagle, Beth Crider-Olcott, Michelle Didesch, Gail Gordon, Mary Ann Gottleib, René Jackson, Stacy Leafgreen, Valerie McCall, Connie Owens, Karla Randle Jackson, Cindy Rocke, Pam Scranton, Kathy Steinheimer, and Valerie Timmes; associate teachers Lynn Akers, Judy Bell, Sue Blasco, Shawna Bradle, Cheryl Breed, Jack Craddock, Julia Graham, Betty Kniss, Cindy Leach, Vicki Lockhart, Kathy Nordvall, Valerie Ray, Tammy Shinkey, and Wendy Smith; family program faculty and staff members Marta Butler, Debra Fisher, Barbara Gordon, Elaine Greer, Maxene Harris, Lorraine Harvey, Judith Hurt, Paula Osborn, and Pat Perry; specialized faculty and staff Janni Bevenour, Meredith Borin, Pam Doloszychi, Kelly Fandell, Nancy Higgins, and Ella Norris; and staff members Leola Clark, Chris Deluhery, Angie Hogan, William Lewis, Lyle Meece, Cynthia Mitchell, Fredesvinda Olson, and Bill Patten.

I also wish to acknowledge Bradley University Dean Joan L. Sattler, College of Education and Health Sciences, and my department chair, Dr. Lori Russell-Chapin, for supporting my work and providing the sabbatical that made finishing this book possible; Christine J. Villani, Monmouth University, for helpful reviews of the manuscript and for being a stimulating and supportive Bradley faculty colleague throughout the project; Nel Noddings, for encouraging me to develop my research into a book; Roland S. Barth, for contributing the Foreword; Robert Sylwester, University of Oregon, for reviewing the brain research implications developed in Chapter 7; Rosalyn Anstine Templeton, Bradley University, for helpful dialogue about caring as an aspect of a learning environment; Heljä Robinson and Bob Wolffe, Bradley University, for sharing resources and refining my understanding of how caring enhances learning; Paul Holmes, Director of Research, Evaluation, and Testing for Peoria Public Schools, and Jim Martindale, Illinois State University, for analysis and interpretation of the learning outcomes data presented in Chapter 7; Brian Ellerbeck and Amy Detjen, Teachers College Press, for superb and caring editing; Jamie R. Burton, for diligent research into the history of Southtown; Jean V. Osterman, for transcribing tapes of my Hinton interviews; Florence McGuire Roe, my enthusiastic aunt, who believed in the project and read the early drafts; Margo Lyman Thompson, for support only a sister can offer;

Linda J. Ging, for listening and a lifetime of friendship; Burton and Doris Lyman, my now-deceased parents, for passing on to me their love of learning; my children—David Gale, for caring that runs deep, Steve Gale, for unwavering love and reminding me to play, and Elaine Gale, my writer daughter, for loyal love and exuberant pride; and finally, Jette a'Porta, for abiding love and partnership.

◄§ 1 §►

Why Care About Caring?

The circle is nature's most perfect form. To the Dakota/Lakota and other Indian tribes, the circle is a sacred symbol of life. . . . Individual parts within the circle connect with every other; and what happens to one, or what one part does, affects all within the circle.
—Virginia Driving Hawk Sneve, "Women of the Circle"

ON A STARKLY COLD night, the last evening in January 1996, a circle of parents took my understanding of caring in schools to a new level. The gathering of 14 parents started inauspiciously following sandwiches, coffee, and cookies. They had come by invitation to talk with the principal of the Valeska Hinton Early Childhood Education Center in Peoria, Illinois. The setting for what became an extraordinary conversation was a room about the size of a kindergarten classroom, but furnished like a living room with comfortable sofas and chairs, end tables, and softly lit lamps. After hearing his brief opening welcome, the parents informally discussed a whole range of topics with the principal, Ken Hinton. Concerns about sibling rivalry alternated with questions about the program change soon to be under way. Families wanted more information about why the multiage K-1 classrooms would be separating into kindergarten and first grade rooms. An easy give-and-take ensued as parents dialogued with Hinton and one another about parenting, the program, and their children's progress.

Hinton scheduled the series of classroom meetings with families because knowing and speaking with parents about their children is important to him. Toward the end of the hourlong meeting Hinton addressed each person in the circle and asked about each child. Eventually he came to a young woman sitting alone on one of the couches, looking quite pensive. "And how is Jason?" he asked. Her quick reply conveyed serious discouragement. "Oh, he is just a demon child," she said without a smile. Immediately, other parents began responding. The comments of several parents confirmed that Jason was a handful. Each seemed to know a story about him that demonstrated either problems or progress in his behaviors. One mother, a regular volunteer in Jason's classroom, described their developing relationship and his growing willingness to cooperate, to do what she asked. Speaking earnestly, she explained why she looked forward to spending time with him. "Jason is my special classroom project," she said. "I think he is improving every day." The genuine outpouring of communal empathy reassured the sadly discouraged young mother.

After telling several stories of his own early misbehaviors, Hinton encouraged the parents always to be positive with their children, never to give up on them. Speaking first about his own mother's influence on him, he then shared the story of a remarkable African American neurosurgeon, Benjamin Carson. Carson became a doctor because of the love and encouragement of his mother, a woman who had only a third grade education herself. Hearing that story, the mother who had spoken so positively about her work with Jason confessed to feeling bad about her own lack of education. "I wish I had not dropped out of high school. I just don't know enough," she said. "I feel so dumb when my daughter asks me something and I don't know the answer. Then she says, 'Why don't you know, Mommy?'" Seeming to know her well, Hinton responded warmly, "Of course you know things, important things. Besides, I remember when you were a great student in my eighth grade social studies class. It's not too late to continue your education. I know you will go back." Having affirmed her ability, he turned his attention to the whole group, closing the meeting by complimenting all the parents on taking responsibility for each other's children. "Your children are learning about caring from watching you," he said.

When I began my exploration of how a principal contributes to building a caring environment, I anticipated finding that teachers and other staff members would also be integral to a caring school. I had not expected to find parents so actively involved in knowing and caring for each other's children. By both requiring and welcoming their involvement in the classrooms, as well as a host of other activities, the faculty and staff have drawn the parents into the circle of caring and recreated the reality of another time when neighbors knew each other and watched out for each other's children.

PORTRAIT WITH A PURPOSE

My original purpose in undertaking a qualitative case study of a caring leader was to chronicle and analyze the contributions to a school's environment of a principal whose leadership is grounded in care for students, families, teachers, and the community. I chose the particular principal and school because, as one former teacher put it, "Ken Hinton epitomizes caring." Although a fledgling connoisseur, I recognized him to be the quintessential caring principal. I was eager to observe him in action, suspecting that his way of leading was central to the Valeska Hinton Early Childhood Education Center's unique environment. My research began in September 1995. The intensive initial research period lasted six months, with ongoing observations, document collection and analysis, and interviews concluding in June 1998.

My interest in the subject has been both practical and theoretical. Practically, I sought a deepened understanding of the complexities and possibilities of caring school leadership to enlighten my teaching of prospective principals. Theoretically, I wanted to test the theories about caring school leadership against the practice. Having an intuitive grasp of the importance of caring leadership, I needed to develop an intellectual understanding to match. Eventually the scope of the project broadened, and I envisioned a portrait of a caring principal, an in-depth many-layered description of good leadership and an inspirational mirror for those who would lead with care. My approach to both the research and writing blends the methods of inquiry developed by Eisner (1991) and Lawrence-Lightfoot and Davis (1997). My goal as a writer is to present an engaging, interpretive, analytical portrait of a caring leader, a portrait of goodness that will invite readers to reflect.

A Caring Principal

Kenneth H. Hinton was appointed director/principal of the Valeska Hinton Early Childhood Education Center in November 1992, at age 46. Located in central Illinois, Peoria's population of approximately 115,000 is included in a larger metropolitan service area population of approximately 349,000. At the time of his appointment Hinton was principal of Harrison Primary School, a Pre-K–4 building attended by students who live in Harrison Homes, one of three public housing projects for low-income families. A full page of text and pictures in the local newspaper described his last day at Harrison: "It was the Friday before Thanksgiving, and the children at Harrison School had little to give thanks for. In small assemblies in the school gym, class by class, children sobbed as Ken Hinton told them it was his last day as their school principal" (Howard, 1992, p. B7). In small groups, he read to all the children an open letter, addressed "To my dear and most beloved children," believing the news would be well received if he explained in person why he was leaving to become director of Peoria's new early childhood center. Still, children and even some faculty cried because, in the words of a second grade teacher, "He loves children. He is support- ive and caring about everyone. He's a wonderful man and we will all miss him. The children seem to know he (Hinton) is one-in-a-million, and they are losing him" (Howard, 1992, p. B7). Figure 1.1 shows Harrison children and Hinton in a hug that displays mutual affection.

A Caring School

At the time of Hinton's appointment, the Valeska Hinton Early Childhood Education Center building was under construction, program development was incomplete, and staff were yet to be selected. This public school, de- signed to be a national model, was the result of a three-year planning and collaboration process involving the Peoria public schools, the City of Peoria Public Building Commission, local businesses, the community college,

Figure 1.1. Children hug Ken Hinton on his last day as principal of Harrison Primary School. Photo by Fred Zwicky/*Peoria Journal Star*.

universities, and other early childhood programs in the city, including Head Start, YMCA, the Urban League, and other child care centers. Well-known early childhood specialists Dr. Lilian Katz of the University of Illinois and Dr. Barbara T. Bowman of the Erikson Institute of Chicago were consultants to the project. Hinton's leadership guided the final phases of development, staffing, and implementation of the school's program. He has been a principal in the Peoria public schools since 1987. Considered an urban school district, Peoria public schools in the fall of 1998 enrolled 16,018 students and employed 1,225 certified staff members, including 37 full-time principals. According to the 1997–98 low-income and racial/ethnic enrollment reports, 58% of the students were from low-income families and 56.51% were members of minority groups. African Americans constitute the school district's largest minority group, 52.77%, although they account for a much smaller percentage of Peoria's population, only 20.87% according to the 1990 census.

My initial research took place from September 1995 through February 1996, during the school's third full year of service to approximately 375 children organized into preprimary (3- and 4-year-olds) and primary (5- and 6-year-olds) multiage groups. The student selection team chooses children and families for the school through an admission process that involves a variety of criteria and considers applicants from the entire community. Funding requires that a majority of the student population be from low-income families. Families consent to significant participation and benefit from multiple educational opportunities and support services, including an on-site Family Health Center. The school operates on a 12-month calendar, giving children the equivalent of a 9-month school year by following a continuous cycle of 9 weeks in session and 3 weeks off. Every facet of the school and its program displays early childhood education best practices.

BUILDING A THEORETICAL FRAME

To conduct meaningful inquiry into caring leadership required developing a more comprehensive personal understanding of the meanings of caring. I soon discovered that neither *care* nor *caring* are easily defined. Beck and Newman (1996) comment succinctly on how caring's multiple meanings "make defining, recognizing, and conducting research on it quite challenging" (p. 172), encouraging openness "to the possibility that caring takes many forms and has many faces" (p. 172). My conceptual understanding of caring deepened and evolved throughout the inquiry process from the interplay between readings and reflective observations. I present my thinking about the meaning and significance of caring in this introduction to clarify my biases, construct a frame, and give the portrait a theoretical context.

Mayeroff: Caring's Purpose

Mayeroff's (1971) *On Caring* provided an entry into the complexity of caring. Mayeroff offers a clear statement of caring's purpose in a definition that is singularly compatible with education: "To care for another person, in the most significant sense, is to help him grow and actualize himself" (p. 1). The book's two related themes, Mayeroff explains, are "a generalized description of caring and an account of how caring can give comprehensive meaning and order to one's life" (p. 2). As part of the generalized description, he identifies the following pattern of interaction as basic to caring:

> I experience the other as an extension of myself and also as independent and with the need to grow; I experience the other's development as bound up with my own sense of well-being; and I feel needed by it for that growing. I respond affirmatively and with devotion to the other's need, guided by the direction of its growth. (p. 6)

Caring as the facilitation of growth requires devotion to the other, Mayeroff insists, and "when devotion breaks down, caring breaks down" (p. 5). The straightforward purpose of helping another grow is immediately complicated for many by issues of process and control. Mayeroff remains clear, however, that caring is never about imposing direction or dominating, a position with implications for principals.

The second theme of Mayeroff's book is that caring gives meaning and purpose to one's whole life. He writes: "Caring has a way of ordering activities around itself; it becomes primary and other activities and values come to be secondary" (p. 37). He also asserts that caring must be rooted in the caring individual's "distinctive powers" (p. 41). Only when our caring emerges from who we are as individual persons can caring relationships center us in the world, cause us to be "in place" or at home (p. 39), he believes. His coupling of *caring as the promotion of growth* with *centeredness* magnifies the potential value of caring in schools for both educators and students, whatever their ages. For educators, answering "Why care about caring?" could stop with Mayeroff.

Gilligan: Caring's Orientation

Gilligan's (1982) *In a Different Voice* examines care as a value and an ethical orientation. These ideas emerge in the context of her exploration of women's development of a moral voice. She suggests that there are two distinct voices in conversations about morality. Gilligan characterizes these as male and female voices that "typically speak of the importance of different truths, the former of the role of separation as it defines and empowers the self, the latter of the ongoing process of attachment that creates and sustains the human community" (p. 156). Gilligan describes one voice, typically but not necessarily male, as speaking from an ethic of justice. She describes the other voice, typically but not necessarily female, as resonating with an ethic of care. The voice concerned with justice speaks from a concern with fairness, equality, rules and regulations uniformly enforced, whereas "an ethic of care rests on the premise of nonviolence—that no one should be hurt" (p. 174). Inasmuch as she identifies caring with women and justice with men, Gilligan casts caring as gender related. By implication, her work raises the question of whether men in leadership positions can be caring. Caring implies flexibility and a certain nonconformity to arbitrary rules, she also seems to suggest. Because bureaucratic schools typically are ordered through a principal's uniform enforcement of rules and regulations, two other questions are raised by Gilligan's analysis: Can principals care, and can schools be caring environments?

Noddings: Caring's Path

Noddings (1984) begins *Caring* with three dictionary definitions of care: "That 'care' is a state of mental suffering or of engrossment: to care is to be in a burdened mental state, one of anxiety, fear, or solicitude about something or someone" (p. 9); second, that "one cares for something or someone if one has a regard for or inclination toward that something or someone" (p. 9); and finally, "to care may mean to be charged with the protection, welfare, or maintenance of something or someone" (p. 9). Noddings builds on Gilligan's work and echoes her distinction between justice and care when she writes that "to care is to act not by fixed rule but by affection and regard" (1984, p. 24). Noddings describes caring's path as existing always in relationships, as involving both a *one-caring* and a one *cared-for*.

Noddings (1984) does not simplify caring. She methodically discusses caring's paradoxes throughout an analysis that only seems to complicate our understanding of this deceptively simple word. Focusing first on behaviors of the one-caring, Noddings argues that *action* and *engrossment* are key components of caring. Action, she writes, is "directed toward the welfare, protection, or enhancement of the cared-for" (p. 23), and engrossment is defined as being present in the acts of caring, conveying "regard, a desire for the other's well-being" (p. 19). Essentially, one's attention or "mental engrossment is on the cared-for, not on ourselves" (p. 24). Noddings writes:

> As we examine what it means to care and to be cared for, we shall see that both parties contribute to the relation; my caring must somehow be completed in the other if the relation is to be described as caring. (1984, p. 4)

Calling this phenomenon *reciprocity*, Noddings identifies it as a third key component of caring. "The cared-for responds to the presence of the one-caring" (p. 60), Noddings explains. Partly that happens because of the "attitude of warm acceptance and trust [that] is important in all caring relationships" (p. 65), she asserts. Caring only exists when the cared-for responds somehow, although that response can take a variety of forms (p. 74).

Other scholars consider and refer to Gilligan and Noddings when studying caring. For example, Eaker-Rich, Van Galen, and Timothy (1996) differentiate the ideas of Gilligan and Noddings, writing that, "Gilligan's early work warns against the inaccuracies of equating care with feelings as opposed to thought, and she names care as an orientation. Noddings construed caring as a process located in education" (p. 233). Both Gilligan and Noddings connect caring with women's ways of speaking and being, this link possibly limiting interest in caring as a significant component of leadership. Noddings has written, however, "For my part, although I haven't been as clear as I should have been, I identify caring with women's experience (as historical fact) but do not want to limit caring to women. Your case study of Hinton is most welcome in this connection" (personal communication, November 21, 1996). Noddings's (1992) argument that "the traditional organization of schooling is intellectually and morally inadequate for contemporary society" (p. 173) calls on male and female educational leaders to care, to abandon bureaucratic inflexibility, and to commit to development of students' academic, social, and emotional capabilities.

Caring School Leaders Make a Difference

Lawrence-Lightfoot (1983), Beck (1994a, 1994b), and Dillard (1995) complete the theoretical framing of Hinton's portrait from a fourth perspective, studies of caring school leaders who make a difference.

Lawrence-Lightfoot: Caring and Goodness. Although designed to display the goodness of the schools and their leaders, Lawrence-Lightfoot's (1983) classic portraits of six good high schools also illuminate caring in the leadership of the principals, all of whom were men. Calling for consideration of whether schools are *good* rather than whether they are *effective*, Lawrence-Lightfoot writes that "the six portraits in this book illustrate the countless ways in which administrators, teachers, and students combine to form a community" (p. 346). In these schools students had a strong sense of belonging. They felt that "their individual actions made a difference to the life of the school," and they had a "sense of being visible and accounted for" (p. 348). In these schools students also felt safe, physically and psychologically. Lawrence-Lightfoot foreshadows brain researchers' emphasis on the relationship between learning and the emotions, asserting that "[u]nless the school environment feels safe and secure they will not be able to focus on matters of the mind" (p. 356). Directly addressing protective caring as an aspect of good schools, Lawrence-Lightfoot observes that "a final way of judging institutional goodness for students is to observe the regard and treatment of the weakest members" (p. 349). She then recalls "vivid examples of this care and concern for the weakest members" (p. 349).

Lawrence-Lightfoot was one of the first to boldly disregard the effective schools rhetoric, interpreting the portraits she created through a different lens. "My descriptions of good high schools were, of course, shaped by my views on institutional goodness—a broader, more generous perspective than the one commonly used in the literature on 'effective' schools" (p. 23). She writes of goodness as an ethos, a complicated quality arising from a constellation of factors, including caring. She documents how in these schools the "students experience the caring, individualized attention of 'humanistic' education" (p. 23). The goodness she portrays incorporates a caring that is more than protective. Lawrence-Lightfoot broadens the implication that caring is a component of good leadership with these words: "We discover that the qualities traditionally identified as female—nurturance, receptivity, responsiveness to relationships and context—are critical to the expression of a non-caricatured masculine leadership" (p. 25). Lawrence-Lightfoot's understanding of caring aligns with Mayeroff's (caring as nurturance) and Noddings's (caring is in relationships). Seeing female qualities as critical to authentic noncaricatured masculine leadership, Lawrence-Lightfoot melds the gender-identified ethical orientations developed by Gilligan. Hinton's example also illustrates a noncaricatured masculine leadership.

Beck: Caring and Transformation. Beck's (1994a) profile of a principal she calls Mary Story focuses directly on caring leadership. Story transformed a complex multiethnic troubled school in the Los Angeles community of Watts into a caring community during her seven-year tenure. Beck concludes that the principal transformed the school because she "embraced the complexity of the situation in which she found herself, surfaced conflict and handled it constructively, and evidenced a long-term commitment" (p. 190) to the community. Beck's concept of emotional investment echoes Mayeroff's devotion and Noddings's engrossment. Emphasizing that commitment is an integral part of caring leadership, Beck writes:

> It is this commitment that moves caring beyond a response or behavior conditioned on something another does into the realm of unconditional acceptance. If one truly cares, she or he will remain emotionally invested in relationships, committed to the others regardless of changing circumstances. (p. 199)

In *Reclaiming Educational Administration as a Caring Profession* (1994b), Beck further defines caring's purposes, context, and activities while providing deontological and consequentialist arguments for a caring ethic. Providing a synthesis of various theoretical perspectives and reflecting on caring's significance for school leaders, Beck asserts that the ethic and practice of caring leadership can help schools meet three important challenges: improving academic performance, battling social problems, and rethinking organizational strategies. Beck reports cynical responses from colleagues to her research on the subject of caring in educational administration, giving as one example, "'Caring and educational administrators—That's really an oxymoron'" (p. 131). Nevertheless, Beck proposes that all administrators should care about caring and has constructed a broad overview of caring in educational administration. She formulates three labels to describe possible roles of a caring educational leader: "(1) values-driven organizer; (2) capable and creative pedagogue; and (3) cultivator of a caring culture" (p. 78). Although Ken Hinton is all of those, roles and labels do not describe him. Rather, his life and work illustrate Noddings's (1992) statement that "caring is a way of being in relation, not a set of specific behaviors" (p. 17).

Dillard: Caring and Diversity. Dillard's (1995) portrait of an African American urban high school principal also describes a caring school leader. Combining African American, feminist, and critical theory perspectives, Dillard presents Gloria Natham as a principal whose leadership reinterprets and authenticates. Dillard writes that Natham "nurtures—and leads—by her presence, by her example, by the way she conducts her life and work in 'putting herself on the line for them'" (p. 557). She speaks and acts authoritatively to require ambivalent parents and teachers to support the achievement of African American students. Dillard writes that "we have much to learn from the ways in which Natham (re)created an environment of care for students" (pp. 559–69). She concludes that a "tenet of effective leadership in diverse ethnic and cultural group settings holds that concern, care, and advocacy for the individual needs of students is critical" (p. 559). Although perceived as caring, Dillard's authoritative style stands in sharp contrast to Hinton's congenial friendliness. For both of these principals, however, the purpose of caring is the same and is reminiscent of Mayeroff. Caring is about helping the students have what they need to develop their full potential as human beings.

Summary

Giving shape, texture, and substance to the theoretical frame are four perspectives: caring both *gives* and *is* purpose (Mayeroff, 1971); caring is an ethical orientation (Gilligan, 1982); caring is a relational process involving engrossment, action, and reciprocity (Noddings, 1984); and caring leaders make a difference. *How* caring leaders make a difference colors the fourth perspective: caring leaders who protect and nurture are critical to maintaining schools that are good (Lawrence-Lightfoot, 1983); leaders grounded in an ethic of caring transform schools by embracing complexity and making an emotional investment (Beck, 1994a, 1994b); and caring leaders who advocate for the needs of individual students are critical to students' success, particularly in culturally diverse schools (Dillard, 1995). A reading of this multilayered portrait in words will reveal that Hinton's caring is both a purpose and a source of meaning, as well as an ethical orientation and a way of being in relationships. To understand how his uncommon caring makes a difference is the most important reason to read this book. My premise is that every person has the potential for uncommon caring.

SIGNIFICANCE OF CARING LEADERSHIP

Caring leadership builds a learning community that includes everyone involved with a school. From a variety of disciplines, scholars are suggesting directly or by implication that the presence or absence of caring affects, and some say determines, the degree of learning in schools (Barth, 1990; Caine & Caine, 1991, 1997; Damasio, 1994; Sergiovanni, 1994; Sylwester, 1995; LeDoux, 1996; Greenspan, 1997; Elias et al., 1997; Jensen, 1998). For example, Sylwester (1995) reports that recent research on brain processes has verified that "emotion is very important to the educative process because it drives attention, which drives learning and memory" (p. 72). He suggests the importance of a caring environment to learning, writing that "emotionally stressful school environments are counterproductive because they can reduce the students' ability to learn" (p. 77).

At the same time and also from a variety of perspectives, persons serious about reforming education are advocating a renewed emphasis on caring school leadership (Kohn, 1991, 1996; Starratt, 1991, 1996; Noblit, 1993a, 1993b; Sergiovanni, 1991; Noddings, 1992; Beck, 1994a, 1994b; Quint, 1994; Dillard, 1995; Lipsitz, 1995; Epstein, 1995; Newburg, 1995; Rossi & Stringfield, 1995; Lewis, Schaps, & Watson, 1995; Kratzer, 1996; Ryan & Friedlaender, 1996; Marshall, Patterson, Rogers, & Steele, 1996). For example, Marshall et al. (1996) argue "that a radically different perspective on leadership, an ethic of caring, is needed if our purpose as educators is to nurture children and to teach them to be caring, moral, productive members of society" (p. 272). They assert:

> With the exception of Beck's [citations omitted] recent work, the writing, teaching, and theory of administration are silent about how to incorporate caring with leadership. . . . No mainstream texts on educational administration and no formal recruitment, training, and selection policies validate the caring perspective. (p. 289)

Arguing for this silence to be broken, they suggest that "for students and teachers to be connected to their schools, indeed for learning to occur, educational administrators' behavior must be centered on caring" (p. 291).

How Do They Know You Care? is a response to the silence in mainstream educational administration texts on caring as a significant component of school leadership for men as well as women. Focus on a male principal illustrates that caring administrators are indeed male as well as female. For men who dismiss caring leadership as a woman's way of leading, nice but not necessary, my hope is that Hinton's example will further degender both the construct and the practice of caring leadership. Caring is foundational, the source of community and the ground of our common humanity whatever our gender, race, or ethnicity.

A case study is a type of qualitative investigation that focuses on the particular through "examination of a specific phenomenon such as a program, a person, a process, an institution, or a social group" (Merriam, 1988, p. 9). I have observed, investigated, and analyzed the uncommon caring of a particular school leader. My report, written in the first person, is built from my interpretation of what I have seen and heard (Eisner, 1991). Working from principles of qualitative research throughout this three-year inquiry (Glaser & Strauss, 1967; Bogdan & Biklen, 1982; Lincoln & Guba, 1985; Merriam, 1988; Wolcott, 1990; Eisner, 1991; Seidman, 1991; Coffey & Atkinson, 1996; Lawrence-Lightfoot & Davis, 1997), my intent is to create a fully developed portrait of an uncommonly caring leader, a portrait that is more than idiosyncratic, a mirror of goodness.

I am guided not by classical conceptions of generalization, but by the belief of qualitative researchers well expressed by Lawrence-Lightfoot and Davis (1997), that "in the particular resides the general" (p. 14). Lawrence-Lightfoot writes:

> The portraitist seeks to document and illuminate the complexity and detail of a unique experience or place, hoping the audience will see themselves reflected in it, trusting that the readers will feel identified. The portraitist is very interested in the single case because she believes that embedded in it the reader will discover resonant universal themes. (in Lawrence-Lightfoot & Davis, 1997, p. 14)

The reader can expect to view the various contexts that shape the subject of the portrait, to experience my relationship with the subject in the clarity of my voice, and to watch details and patterns become a complex completed canvas that depicts a whole, believable person. If this portrait of uncommon caring is successful, it will be persuasive, an aesthetic whole with a meaning larger than the life of an individual person (Eisner, 1991; Lawrence-Lightfoot & Davis, 1997). If the work is to have meaning for individual readers, Hinton's story must resonate, must echo in the crevices and caverns of the mind, and must raise important questions to be considered within the context of one's own life, professional practices, and aspirations. Resonance both stimulates and requires reflection.

Caring by those in leadership positions is underresearched partly because caring seems to defy definition. Caring leadership has been undervalued as well as superficially understood. Politicians' emphasis on accountability, promoted by standards and measured by achievement test scores, continues to undermine the singular importance of caring in the development of children and their learning. Furthermore, the absence of caring leadership practices is too often accepted as commonplace by those comfortable with bureaucratic schools. If caring affects learning and every other aspect of school life, then the practices and challenges of caring leadership must be understood by those who would lead good schools well. The significance of leadership grounded in caring is its power to transform schools into more humane places. If uncommon caring were commonplace in schools, barriers of difference would be dissolved, circles of community would be rebuilt, and schools would become welcoming learning environments for all.

A question and answer conclude this introduction: "Why should we care about caring? Because without caring, individual human beings cannot thrive, communities become violent battlegrounds, the American democratic experiment must ultimately fail, and the planet will not be able to support life" (Lipsitz, 1995, p. 665). This dramatic claim is one approach to the societal significance of caring leadership. On a personal level as educators, caring's claim on our attention can begin with the evidence that young persons who experience caring grow stronger. Indeed, they have a better chance of learning and of becoming caring persons themselves.

"Individual parts within the circle connect with every other; and what happens to one, or what one part does, affects all within the circle" (Sneve, 1986, p. 130). We recreate the circle of community as we care, one person at a time. The reciprocal cycle of caring requires our engrossment and our actions. However, as parents, teachers, and school leaders we must each care in ways that are uniquely our own, realizing that caring emerges from the ground of who we are, moves from inside out, or else it moves no one.

QUESTIONS FOR PERSONAL REFLECTION

How might my leadership be changed by a deeper understanding of caring?

What part does caring play in my life's purposes?

Is caring as a value included in my ethical beliefs?

To what extent do I engage in and foster caring relationships?

Am I a leader who makes a difference?

⊸ς 2 ς➤

Southtown's Homegrown Principal

Like all researchers working within the phenomenological framework, por-
traitists find *context* crucial to their documentation of human experience
and organizational culture. By context, I mean the setting—physical, geographic, temporal, historical, cultural, aesthetic—within which the action
takes place. Context becomes the framework, the reference point, the map,
the ecological sphere; it is used to place people and action in time and
space and as a resource for understanding what they say and do. The context is rich in clues for interpreting the experience of the actors in a setting. . . . The description works from the outermost circle inward, macro to
micro, large to small, backdrop to foreground, general to specific, public
to private. We see a sketch of the city, then move to the neighborhood,
then to the school filled with individuals.
—Sara Lawrence-Lightfoot, "Illumination: Framing the Terrain"

THE WORK OF LEADERSHIP always exists within a particular setting. Rendering a word portrait of a leader requires making that setting clear. My
description of the context of Hinton's leadership will move, as Lawrence-
Lightfoot suggests, "from the outermost circle inward" (in Lawrence-
Lightfoot & Davis, 1997, p. 45), beginning in this chapter with community,
neighborhood, and family. Visiting the Valeska Hinton Early Childhood
Education Center requires for me a downhill journey of only a few blocks, a
drive I have made countless times from Bradley University on the hilltop to
the Southtown neighborhood in the valley. From the campus, I follow curv-
ing University Street, which becomes MacArthur Highway as soon as it
crosses Moss Avenue, a street of historic homes and mansions built along
the bluff. Peoria's early wealthy residents built these homes to escape from
the stifling heat of the Illinois River valley in summer. Downtown Peoria
today still sits in the valley along the river's western bank, where the water
is wide like a lake. The city extends in either direction along the river, running into Bartonville on the southwest and extending to the north up the
bluffs to Peoria Heights. The wide middle of the city fans out for about 10
miles north to where it borders the sprawling suburban area called Dunlap.

I turn left at the bottom of the long hill and pull into the school's parking lot. The Valeska Hinton Center nestles attractively in the valley at the end of the river flatlands, under the shadow of the bluffs. I look in four directions. To the west of the school and its grounds is MacArthur Highway, down which I have driven. The street serves as the western boundary of this area called Southtown. South of the school and edging the entire length of the school's busy parking lot is a newly refurbished park area, complete with a children's play area, a water park, tennis courts, baseball diamonds, and basketball courts. Visible beyond the park is the George Washington Carver Community Center, a longtime feature and hub of Southtown. To the east is a large church, a street, and vacant land. Across the street in front of the school, to the north, is an expanse of land with rows of mature shade trees. One can clearly see where houses stood before urban renewal. Now the area is fenced and gated, called Spring Grove when begun by its developer in 1994. A handful of new homes are occupied, with several others in various stages of construction. After the groundbreaking for the new residential development, a Southtown community activist spoke: "The garment of destiny is finally being woven in the fiber and fabrics of Southtown transforming as Dr. [Martin Luther] King once said, 'the dark yesterdays into the bright tomorrows'" (Allen, 1994, p. 1). I wonder if any Native American from the Peoria tribe ever stood on this ground, paid homage to the four directions, and looked to the future.

CONTEXTS OF COMMUNITY, NEIGHBORHOOD, AND FAMILY

To understand the Ken Hinton I have come to know, one must consider his story in the contexts of community, neighborhood, and family. The community is Peoria, the oldest European settlement in Illinois. The neighborhood is Southtown. When Hinton was born in 1946 his family lived in the heart of Southtown. His home was about 500 feet away from where the Valeska Hinton Early Childhood Education Center is now located. The family lived at that address until Hinton was five, then moved three blocks down the street. When Hinton married, he moved only a block away from his parents' home. This is the setting, "physical, geographic, temporal, historical, cultural, aesthetic" (Lawrence-Lightfoot & Davis, 1997, p. 41), that has both shaped and claimed Hinton and his talents. His home today, however, is not located in Southtown or even within the city limits of Peoria. Similarly, his imagination and vision have never been limited by boundaries of race or place.

Layers of Community History

Peoria occupies the spot in central Illinois where, in the words of a Peoria enthusiast, "valley, bluff and river combine to form a location of such spectacular beauty and natural abundance as to make the location of Peoria, from the beginning of time, quite inevitable" (Klein, 1985, p. 11). Archaeologists have traced evidence of early humans in the Peoria area as far back as 10,000 B.C.E. In the mid-1600s the river valley was a favorite winter fishing and hunting ground for nomadic tribes, chiefly Illinois Indians. Beginning in 1673, French explorers entered the area, and although Peoria was a French settlement for 131 years, today almost no traces of French Peoria remain. The settlement survived until 1812, when an American expedition dispatched against the Indians located in the area turned into a looting and burning spree that destroyed the still predominantly French village (Klein, 1985, p. 48).

By the early 1830s the town, now officially named Peoria after the largest tribe of the Illinois nation, consisted of 21 log cabins and 7 frame houses. The settlement grew as the steamboat trade, slaughterhouses, and breweries flourished. During the 1890s, Peoria was on the circuit for variety acts on their way to vaudeville; hence the "Will it play in Peoria?" question that still lingers over the city's reputation. The contention of critics was that success before Peoria's discriminating audiences predicted success on the country's larger stages. After surviving the depression and weathering the war, the formerly bustling Peoria downtown began to decline in the 1950s as the move to the suburbs of people and shopping happened throughout the country. According to Klein, "This became almost a ghost town, with empty and littered streets and crumbling pavement" (1985, p. 93). Peoria's historical layers suggest a community that more than once has become either a literal or virtual ghost town before enjoying rejuvenation and rebirth.

In 1840 there were 8 African Americans in Peoria; by 1850 the number had risen to 84, and by 1860 the number was 109 (Garrett, 1973, p. 78). Before the Civil War both pro- and antislavery agitation occurred in Peoria, with the home of a prominent citizen playing an important role as a depot on the Underground Railroad. In 1856 a school for African Americans opened, and special schools were maintained until African Americans integrated into the public schools in 1871. De facto segregation developed over time, however, based on the restriction of African Americans to certain areas of housing, mostly in Southtown. Integration officially happened for the second time almost 100 years later when the Board of Education began a busing program in 1968. The first African American church in Peoria was the Ward A.M.E. Chapel, founded in 1846. Its present church building is located across the street from the Valeska Hinton Center, at the western edge of the Spring Grove housing development. To understand Hinton's reality as an African American in Peoria, one must consider the history of Southtown.

Confines of the Southtown Neighborhood

To Hinton's family, living in Southtown, *neighborhood* meant "your own side of the block." Hinton's parents did not allow him to cross the street as a child. He was effectively "locked in" without gates. Hinton remembers sitting during lazy summer days on a backyard bench built by his father and wishing fervently to go across the street. Permission to do that came later, at about age 14, although when he was 11 or 12 he could ride his bicycle alongside the curb up and down the block. Even walking to school was along a certain path, he said:

> That's the way you walked, and that's the way you came back, and you wouldn't venture to the park, to the store, or anywhere else unless you were given permission. It was a good neighborhood, and nobody locked their doors. There was just respect and trust.

The larger Southtown neighborhood encompasses 168 acres, roughly shaped like a diamond, with one of its edges next to the downtown area of Peoria. When Hinton was growing up in the late 1940s and 1950s, families from Southtown's large core group of the African American community all knew or knew of each other. Besides the neighborhood, the African American churches also provided a common ground linking African American families. The Southtown Hinton remembers growing up in was also, however, a multicultural neighborhood including many Lebanese families as well as Germans, Irish, and others. How this richly diverse neighborhood, good for children and families, deteriorated into an area ripe for urban renewal involved the interplay of many factors.

In the late 1940s and early 1950s Caterpillar Inc. began to move uneducated laborers from the South to Peoria to perform the more menial tasks required to keep the factories running smoothly. Some of these persons were Whites, with typical southern attitudes toward African Americans. Seeking housing in Southtown, they added a divisive element to the previously harmonious racial and ethnic mix of people. More of the immigrants were African Americans coming north to the plentiful jobs offered at Caterpillar, "which was a fair employer before Fair Employment Practices Commission was a law in Illinois" (Pugh, 1963a, p. A4). Most of these families also sought housing in Southtown, contributing to the gradual increase in the percentage of African Americans living in the area. According to Pugh, several hundred poor African Americans were dislocated by the 1954 construction of the Taft Homes housing project on the Near North Side site of what was then Peoria's worst slum. Those dislocated also moved into Southtown. Meanwhile, more prosperous White and African American families were leaving Southtown.

President Kennedy's executive order in 1962 calling for an end to discrimination in federally funded housing was big news in Peoria, according to an editorial. It hastened opening of neighborhoods that had "been closed to Negroes because of unwritten real estate laws which have tried to maintain all-white residential areas" ("JFK's Executive Order & Peoria," 1962, p. A-6). As Whites and wealthier African American families no longer restricted by discriminatory housing practices left the area, more African American than White lower-income families, many of whom did not share the neighborhood values, moved into the vacated Southtown homes. Between 1950 and 1970, the African American population of Peoria almost tripled in terms of actual numbers, and doubled in terms of the percentage of the population. According to one observer, the Southtown neighborhood really started to change in 1966 and 1967, and then in 1969 Peoria also experienced, mostly in Southtown, the unrest that followed the death of Dr. Martin Luther King Jr., adding to the public's perception of the neighborhood as an undesirable place to live.

Meanwhile, two years earlier, in 1967, the consulting firm of Vilican-Lehman & Associates presented to the city council a survey of existing conditions in Southtown as part of their proposal for a General Neighborhood Renewal Plan for the Near South Side. The report described the whole neighborhood negatively in these words:

> Being adjacent to the Central Business District, this is one of the oldest residential neighborhoods in the city and it has been subjected to significant social and economic change. The majority of housing is seriously deteriorated and structures are crowded together on lots which are below minimum size required by city zoning ordinances. (*Near South Side General Neighborhood Renewal Plan*, 1967, p. 2)

The consultants acknowledged that some sections of Southtown were in better shape than others. Their plan proposed a series of four urban renewal projects to be completed in phases, stating that these projects "would bring about the general up-grading of the Near South Side and restore it to an attractive residential neighborhood through the elimination of blighted conditions coupled with the rehabilitation and redevelopment of residential, commercial and community facilities" (p. 22). According to the Vilican-Lehman report, the population of Southtown was by then 81.2% non-White.

However, the non-White census designation included "Negroes, Japanese, Chinese, Indians, Filipinos, and so forth" (Pugh, 1963b, p. A1). To conclude a 1963 series on race and housing, *Peoria Journal Star* editor Charles Dancey wrote, "In spite of handicaps of poverty, discrimination and environment there is now the 40 per cent of self-owned, well-kept homes even there. The whole Near South Side doesn't constitute a traditional slum in spite of the age of the housing" (1963, p. A4).

Differing viewpoints about the necessity of the massive urban renewal project eventually adopted persist today, and existed throughout the long debate about whether and how to proceed. Reflection suggests that the urban renewal launched in the late 1960s by the Vilican-Lehman report was as much an effort to remedy the dramatic 1950s decline of downtown Peoria as it was to upgrade living conditions for residents of Southtown. The city officials targeted Southtown for urban renewal because of its proximity to the heart of downtown. The land was valuable for commercial redevelopment purposes, and many saw the prospect of making money. As part of that urban renewal process, 2,000 families lost their homes and their neighborhood.

From Hinton's perspective, when urban renewal was first proposed the Southtown neighborhood was still quite livable. "Papers strewn about, garbage, glass, broken things, houses in ill repair did not exist," he said. Then the city came through in the mid-1960s and told people not to make any major repairs to their homes "because we are going to buy your properties." When the city began to buy properties, the homes were either left vacant to be vandalized or knocked into their basements. Rats, insect infestations, and sewer backups became problems for the remaining residents. These vacated properties were not good for the neighborhood, and general property maintenance deteriorated as anxious people awaited buyouts. In spite of his judgment that the process was badly handled, Hinton evaluates the overall purpose of the project positively, sharing this opinion:

> Its purpose was to revamp the area and put in new homes, new businesses, new industry, but it is only taking place now because then the money and will fell through. The people who were in our community, the people of color, took it very hard because it really destroyed a community, destroyed a way of life.

Over a period of two decades, beginning in 1967 and ending in 1988 or 1989, the city gradually bought and boarded up or tore down homes, eventually leaving only the trees as forlorn markers of what had been a vibrant neighborhood. As a newcomer to Peoria in 1990, I remember driving down MacArthur Highway, seeing only the abandoned trees, and thinking that much of Southtown was virtually a ghost town. Funding difficulties and economic fluctuations also contributed to the delay of the redevelopment process. In the early 1980s, over 10,000 people left Peoria during a widespread Caterpillar Inc. strike, leaving Southtown and other community projects in a holding pattern. According to 1990 U.S. Census Data Files, the overall Peoria population was 124,160 in 1980, but had fallen to 113,504 by 1990. The minority population, however, rose from 22,969 in 1980 to 26,652 in 1990. Meanwhile, in Southtown, as a candidate for a City Council seat stated in a campaign speech criticizing the actions of the politicians, "People are suffering and trapped in an area they don't want to live in because you [City Council members] destroyed everything around there. We must do something. We can't just wait for the economy to turn around" (Hopkins, 1985, p. A7).

Circles of Family

Hinton's father was born to one of the earlier African American families to settle in Peoria. His father's people moved to Peoria at the turn of the century, when there were only 1,402 African Americans in Peoria (Garrett, 1973, p. 78). His mother's father had been a large landholder in southern Illinois, but when the stock market crashed in 1929 he lost everything. Hinton's mother, Cleata Eunice Allen, was the first one from her large family of nine brothers and sisters to move to Peoria, arriving in 1927, with most of the other family members following. Cleata met Hinton's father, Adrian, riding on the trolley to one of the few places where African Americans were allowed to socialize. They were married in 1930. The African American population of Peoria in 1930 was 3,037, or 2.9% of the total population of 104,969 (Garrett, 1973, p. 78).

Cleata and Adrian Hinton had five children, including Adrian Jr., who also was a Peoria public school principal until his untimely death in 1995, and daughters Adrene and LaReta. Ken and his twin sister Marilyn, with Marilyn born first, arrived in 1946 as a surprise to the rest of the children, who had not realized that their mother was pregnant. Ken was also a surprise to his father, who was already on his way out of the hospital when a nurse ran after him to let him know he had another child. Hinton remembers his family being poor and having chickens in the back yard. Hinton's father, one of the two oldest boys in a large family, quit school for work after eighth grade to help his family. He was a hard worker his entire life, never taking a vacation until after his wife's physical therapy business began to prosper.

Hinton's mother, who was a high school graduate, worked hard during the early years of the marriage to take care of her children. She even washed floors at the bus station to help with the family income. When his mother decided to pursue further education, every week during Ken's preschool years Adrian drove her to Chicago, where she earned credentials in physical therapy. After completing the course of study, she turned the family living room into an office and began what became a thriving physical therapy practice that brought the family prosperity. As the business became successful, the family was able to move down the street into a duplex, with one side used for the business. Although poor in Hinton's early years, by 1956 the family was in the upper-middle-class income bracket due to the excellent income earned by his mother.

CAREER AS A CALLING

Hinton has spent more years in school than he planned. He attended four Peoria public schools, all located within or near his Southtown neighborhood home. He remembers always being in the minority as an African American, that a "large number of African American children in my elementary school classrooms would have been maybe five or six." Because of the emotional and economic stability of his family, although he never liked school, no one would have described him as "at risk," Hinton said. In school he found one kind of trial after another, beginning with kindergarten.

Student

Hinton describes his kindergarten experience at Washington School as "difficult." The strict, unsmiling teacher was not inclined to warm relationships with the children. Hinton remembers not wanting to go to school, perhaps because he was so attached to his mother, who was back home after the years of commuting to Chicago. He had other reasons to dislike school, however. He did not like wearing shoes, he was not challenged, and he was always getting into trouble. The teacher sent him home from kindergarten one day because he came to school shoeless, his feet painted black with Esquire shoe polish. The teacher did not realize until midday that he wasn't wearing any shoes, but that was not much consolation as he walked home pondering how to tell his parents. Complicating his kindergarten experience was twin sister Marilyn's habit of telling the teacher everything about what Ken was doing and not doing. In Hinton's words, "The problem was that I would never do what I was supposed to do. I just didn't conform."

Young Ken Hinton simply did not like grade school, and his mind was always someplace else. The culmination of nonconformity came during his sixth grade year at Lincoln School. His parents took him to the fall parent–teacher conference, where he overheard the teacher talk about a standardized test result, telling his parents, "This kid is quite smart!" Ken could not figure that out, since he preferred playing and having fun to doing homework or working in school. What he did figure out was that there was no reason to keep going to school, since he was already smart. He began to get up in the morning and dress for school, but then leave the house to do whatever he wanted. He had a friend who was more than willing to be part of the day's adventures. Together they kept watch for the truant officer as they enjoyed being out of school and about the neighborhood. By then Marilyn no longer told their teachers and parents everything and had settled into a "What will you give me if I don't tell?" relationship with her twin brother.

Because the school did not notify his parents about his absences, Hinton spent much of sixth grade as a chronic truant, to use today's terminology. One of Southtown's most interesting places to Hinton was a pool hall run by the grandparents of Richard Pryor, the comedian. Hinton describes Pop Pryor as a robust guy, old with a very fair complexion, who ran the pool hall with an iron fist. Everyone respected him. There was no trouble, even though smoke rolled out the always open doors and a wide variety of men hung out at the dark, dingy old 1910-style pool hall. It was a place where kids his age always wanted to go, and he was no exception. On a typical day, while his mother offered physical therapy services to her patients, his dad went off to work at Sheridan Road Printing Company in the morning, always carrying a black lunchbox. Once he had driven off in his blue truck, he seldom returned home until after five. Hinton's absences from school ended abruptly the day his dad unexpectedly came home from work during the middle of the afternoon. Driving past the open pool hall door, he saw Ken lingering inside. Hinton describes his father's approach to misbehavior as "from the old school." The reprimand from his father was so severe that from then until he graduated from high school Hinton would have had perfect attendance, except for being deliberately absent several times. From his perspective, to earn a perfect attendance award would have suggested that he liked school when he did not.

At Roosevelt Junior High, Hinton continued what he describes as his engaged behavior. He was well acquainted with the offices and paddles of the principal and assistant principal. All any perceptive teacher had to do, however, was threaten to call his mother or send a note home and he instantly became well behaved. Hinton does not have positive memories of junior high because of how some teachers treated him. For example, he remembers an eighth grade science assignment to draw the human heart. Excited about the project, he got an encyclopedia and colored pencils, staying up practically all night working on the drawing. When the teacher returned his paper the comment was, "Very Good—F." The teacher asked him who drew his picture and called him a liar when he said that he had done it himself. Hinton said, "When we would write essays in class and I'd write my dreams, I'd get F's on those, too, because I was told I copied those out of a book." Repeated experiences like these contributed to Hinton's dislike of school and his growing disinterest. By this age he knew he wanted to become an architect and simply learned anything that interested him on his own time. School he just endured.

Hinton began consistently behaving himself at Manual High School for two reasons: The teachers treated him well, and the consequences of misbehavior became more threatening. Walking by the office one day, he saw through the glass walls the principal swinging a paddle with both hands to administer punishment to a great big football player. At the time Hinton, who weighed 80 pounds and wore a size 3 shoe, decided that such a paddling would kill him. Even though his mischievous adventures continued, from then on he stayed out of the principal's office. Reflecting on his misbehavior, which was more about having fun than causing trouble, Hinton said, "I was a very active kid. My brother was the intellect, and I was the one that said, 'That's not the way for me.'" He understood clearly what kept him out of serious trouble.

> I was not deterred from breaking into a store and getting a new bicycle by the police; nor was I deterred from grabbing a lady's purse, or going to the store and getting candy from the open shelves by the police or other authorities. It was my home. It was my mom and dad. If I were to have the choice of spending the night in jail or dealing with the retribution of my parents I knew I'd take the night in jail.

When Hinton was interested in a class, he challenged himself to earn an A. By the time he was a senior, anything less than a 96 or 97 in history class, for example, he considered a personal failure. He graduated as a member of the first class to have spent their entire senior year at the relocated Manual High School. From seventh grade through high school Hinton took all the mechanical and architectural drafting classes offered, knowing he wanted to become an architect. His mother, however, decreed that he would follow two older siblings up the hill to Bradley University, a school that did not offer architectural drafting. Hinton adjusted by majoring in his other interests, political science and history.

As an African American at Bradley in the 1960s, Hinton continued to have negative classroom experiences. For example, he received a D in freshman English, a class he shared with Marilyn. Whereas he had no trouble with the essay-writing assignments, Marilyn was less well prepared. At the end of the semester the instructor called them both to her desk and said, "I can't fail your sister and give you a B, so I gave you both D's." Another time, when he and Marilyn were in a biology class together, the instructor accused them of cheating because they earned the same number of points in the course and received the same score on an in-class exam. In other classes Hinton remembers doing well on quizzes and exams. Then he would mysteriously receive a different, and lower, final course grade. He did not take his education seriously, the lack of focus resulting from a combination of factors: unfair treatment from teachers, interest in life outside of the classroom, and the responsibilities of marriage and a family.

Hinton started at Bradley in 1964 and was married in 1966, during his sophomore year. He started dating Rita Owens when she was a sophomore in high school and he was a freshman at Bradley. "The first time I saw her I knew I was going to marry her," he said. Although his mother and her father thought they were too young, he was quite persuasive, threatening that they would run away and get married in Missouri. Bowing to their determination, both sets of parents agreed to help the young couple, and they married when Rita was still in high school. Married and still unconvinced of the value of an education, Hinton dropped out of Bradley in 1966 and found a job at Pabst Blue Ribbon. He was told by the man who interviewed him that he would be working in the office.

When Hinton showed up in a suit and tie for work on Monday morning, the office manager had other ideas, telling him he "wasn't working in there," presumably because he was African American. The manager sent him out to unload semi trucks. Several days into the week his supervisor on the dock at Pabst called him over for a little talk. "I see by your information that you've gone to school. You are a damn fool. You need to go to school," he said. Hinton remembers quitting the next day and arranging to return to Bradley. He recalls this man as one of the three persons who most affected his decision to finish his college education. The second person was a Bradley professor who, upon seeing Hinton in the halls again, called him by name and inquired about his having quit. The professor asked Hinton to come talk with him first if he ever thought about quitting one of his classes again. This expression of caring and personal interest by a professor made a significant impression on Hinton. The third person influential in his finishing college was his mother.

By the time Hinton graduated from Bradley midway through the 1968–1969 academic year, he and Rita were the parents of two daughters, MaRita and Aleta. Both working and going to school full time, Hinton fulfilled his promise to his mother to complete college. He graduated in December and planned to begin a position in Washington, D.C. in June. Meanwhile, with a wife and two children to support, he needed a full-time job until then. His mother suggested that he try substitute teaching.

Teacher

Because of his many negative experiences with school, education was never a career option he had considered. Somewhat desperate, however, Hinton decided teaching could be a temporary occupation until June. After obtaining a provisional teaching certificate, Hinton accepted assignment to an eighth grade classroom from which the regular teacher was absent for the rest of the year due to a nervous disorder. The class was so difficult that a series of other substitutes lasting only a day had refused the long-term assignment. Staff from the local juvenile detention center had been filling in to maintain some order until a teacher could be found.

Hinton arrived at the school wearing a white shirt, new suit, and tie. The principal escorted him to the waiting classroom, where a student greeted them at the door, directing these words at Hinton: "We are going to run you out of here." Hearing no response from the principal, Hinton understood what he had to do. When he entered the classroom the next day the class members all started tapping their pencils, making a noise so loud that Hinton was unable to be heard. He sized up the situation and said, "Okay, let me have the biggest, the baddest, and the toughest." Earl Henry, who was bigger than Hinton, volunteered, and the two went outside to a hallway. Hinton said to the boy, "Let me have your best shot," whereby Earl Henry punched him in the face. Then Hinton proceeded to wrestle him to the floor. By the time the fight was over Hinton's tie was off to the side, his watch gone, and his jacket torn. He remembers throwing the boy up against the wall at the end of the fight and remains sure that God's providence kept him from impaling the boy on the coat hooks. Hinton was riled up, emotionally charged, and sure the job was not worth it, but he was determined not to be run out of the classroom. He went back in and said, "Who's next?" Just as the next tough guy stood up, Earl Henry reappeared in the classroom, ordered the kid to "sit your ass down," and then, as Hinton reported to me, "We had class." That was the beginning of his teaching career.

Very shortly Hinton had the class under control and even learning, but members of the group were still misbehaving badly when he was not present. One day he decided to leave a tape recorder running while another teacher taught in the room. Listening later to what had transpired, he asked the principal for permission to suspend the whole class. Permission granted, he suspended them and told them they could not come back to school until they brought their parents. The parents and students arrived the next day, everyone furious with the school and with him. He made a few introductory remarks and then played the taped evidence of the students' foul language and misbehaviors. The anger of the parents turned from Hinton to their children. From that day on, Hinton understood the power of partnership with parents. The students' behavior even for their other teachers dramatically improved. Hinton and the class members became quite close during the few months remaining. He remembers being overcome with emotion when the semester ended in early June. He put his head down on the desk and cried when the class left for the last time. Hinton knew then that he was a teacher and has not regretted the calling of his career.

From 1969 until 1982 Hinton served as an eighth grade teacher at Irving Elementary School. For many of those years he had a second teaching job at what was called "the late-afternoon high school," for children who, due to behavior or attendance issues, were not acceptable in the regular school setting. He was successful with these students, he says, because "I worked with them in a developmental way, not holding them to rigorous high standards, but crediting them with passing when they turned in work and gradually building them toward better quality and self esteem." Many of those who did not ever graduate from high school or go to college are doing well and are productive and good people, he said. Some of these former students have come to him as adults to express their appreciation for his teaching.

Administrator

Central Office administrators encouraged Hinton to think about administration after his first year of teaching, but he was not yet interested. Asked repeatedly to become an administrator, eventually Hinton reached a point where there were things that he wanted to address, to do, and to try that he could not do from within the classroom. Entering administration also meant a higher salary and the opportunity to give up his second teaching position, meaning that he could spend more time with his own family. He and Rita now had five children. A son, Landrian, and daughters MiKelle and Kandace were all born during the years when Hinton was a teacher. He earned an M.A. in secondary education from Bradley in 1971, at the beginning of his career, but delayed earning his administrative credentials until after he was appointed Administrative Assistant at Harrison Elementary School in 1982, serving for four years.

When the district reorganized in 1986, dividing students into primary, middle, and high schools, he was transferred to Trewyn Middle School as an Administrative Assistant. A year later, in 1987, he returned to Harrison Primary School, this time as the principal. With his leadership this troubled school, serving a low-income minority population from the Harrison Homes housing project, became an urban education showcase with large numbers of parents involved, academic achievement rising, and a whole variety of innovative programs in place. The school's direction was altered toward positive academic and behavioral performance. Hinton was successful in changing the community's perception of the school, and instrumental even in modernizing the physical plant.

Speaking to a reporter of his decision to leave Harrison for the Valeska Hinton Center, "'I've got mixed feelings. I love this school, the parents, children, and staff, and that's putting it mildly,' he said. 'But I'm a dreamer. I foresee the early childhood center being one of the best, if not the best, in the nation'" (Howard, 1992, p. B7). Accidentally an educator, Hinton is certainly an example of a person for whom career has been a calling.

KENNETH H. HINTON: A SILHOUETTE

Silhouettes are created by the interplay of light and shadow, positives and negatives. Silhouettes reveal the outlines of a person's shape, but lack the nuances of fully illuminated portraits. My early reflections about Hinton's leadership glimpsed recurring patterns of mind, heart, and action that cast clear shadows of understandings yet to come. Three of these patterns create the silhouette of what will become a full-color rendering of Southtown's homegrown principal as observations, stories, and insights coalesce and come into focus.

Nonconformist

Hinton's behaviors and thoughts as a child were characterized by nonconformity. As an adult, he is still thoughtfully nonconforming. A self-taught teacher, Hinton developed his own methods for reaching challenging students. His first teaching position preceded his formal coursework in education. As a newly appointed administrator, he drew from his own careful observations of veteran principals, his older brother's example, his spiritual beliefs, and a rich background of reading about leaders. Finally given his own building, Hinton did it his way. He went beyond what he had seen in the leadership of others, actualizing his own dreams for children and their families as he and the staff at Harrison Primary School together created innovative programs to promote the learning of a student population considered at risk. To accomplish innovation within a strongly bureaucratic school system, Hinton has more than once practiced forms of creative insubordination. This term first emerged in a major study of Chicago principals conducted in the late 1970s and early 1980s (McPherson & Crowson, 1994) and was thought to be necessary at that time for success in large urban school districts.

His nonconformist habits of mind incline Hinton to innovation. Habitually working from his own learning, he analyzes problematic situations for himself, reads the research, and then works with staff to develop or implement programs that will help children learn. Intrinsically motivated, he trusts his own experience. Hinton resists the constraints of bureaucracy in a variety of ways. For example, in a school district where principals have been more or less directed by Central Office to wear a conventional dark suit and tie if male or a skirted suit or dress if female, he has persisted in being flexible in his approach to dress. Once in a graduate class Hinton was the only person to argue that principals should not always have to wear a tie. When the professor pushed him to justify his opinion, Hinton asked, "Have you ever been grabbed by your tie when you were trying to break up a fight? It can become a lethal weapon." His point was well taken, conceded the professor. As a teacher, some days Hinton wore a tie and some days he did not. This nonconformist pattern has continued to be true in his administrative positions.

An example of nonconformity in Hinton's personal life was the decision to have a commuter marriage for several years. When Rita and Ken had two children in college and three children still at home, Rita accepted a transfer to a position in St. Louis after TWA bought out Ozark Airlines, the company she worked for in Peoria. Rita had taken the position with Ozark in order to contribute financially to the family's growing educational and other expenses. During her three years in St. Louis, Landrian stayed with his father in Peoria to complete his last year of high school. The two youngest girls went to St. Louis with Rita. Being together only on weekends was a difficult sacrifice for the close family. Hinton's custom of putting in long hours at school solidified during this time when he spent much of every week alone, commuting to St. Louis on the weekends.

Some might say that Hinton's nonconformity is typical for a last-born child. Perhaps being the twin of a sister who liked school, as well as the younger brother of the family intellectual, sent him in the direction of nonconformity. Whatever the temperamental or family influences, Hinton's nonconformity and compassion are two equally strong qualities that buttress his leadership.

Compassionate

Compassionate and *caring* are not synonymous, although both words suffer from connotations of excessive sentiment. The noun *compassion* is defined as "a feeling of distress and pity for the suffering or misfortune of another" (McLeod, 1987, p. 195). Synonyms reflect the adjective's full spectrum of meaning. The softer side of *compassionate* is revealed in synonyms such as "indulgent, kind-hearted, kindly, lenient, merciful, pitying, sympathetic, tender, tender-hearted, and understanding." Stronger synonyms for compassionate include "benevolent, charitable, humane, and humanitarian" (McLeod, 1987, p. 197). Hinton's compassion includes both the softer and stronger meanings. My sense is that Hinton's compassion springs from the nurturing he did and didn't receive from his family and the community.

When I inquired about the sources of his understanding of leadership, Hinton described a combination of influences. A voracious reader in seventh and eighth grades, he preferred nonfiction. He read about the lives of real people, many of whom were leaders who overcame tremendous odds. Through books he traveled the world, experienced other realities, and validated his parents' teachings. "My ideal of leadership comes basically from my home and my readings," he explained. "When we were small, before we went to bed, Mother would read stories from the Bible. Whether I realized it at the time or not, that left an impression on me. Then I would see what my mom would do." His mother often did without while doing for others and gave without expecting to receive anything in return. Life in his own home was lived by principles Hinton read about in the lives of great people. His understanding of leadership rests on the pillars of persistence and compassion.

Paradoxically, Hinton's unsatisfying relationship with his father also developed his compassionate nature. Although understanding the influence of his father's age and generation on his parenting style, Hinton confesses to regretting still that he and his father did not have a closer relationship. He would have preferred a father whose ideas about parenting were not "from the old school," to use his words. He would have preferred a doting father. He got a father who was dependable and solid, but rarely warm. Hinton decided early in his own children's lives to be a different kind of father. He resolved not to spank his children, for example. Watching Hinton nurture the needy students who daily seek his hugs and attention, I believe that he regards all children from the perspective of a loving father and gives to them a kind of caring that he did not get from his own father.

Growing up in Peoria as an African American also developed Hinton's compassion. Stories previously recounted from his student experiences illustrate multiple encounters with discrimination. A long list of examples could be constructed, beginning with numerous instances of unfair grading and low expectations from teachers. As a teenager he endured being searched by police when driving the family's Lincoln Continental. Being sent out to unload semi trucks on the dock instead of beginning the promised office job at Pabst seemed clearly discriminatory. A college graduate and employed as a teacher, Hinton was turned down for a bank loan in the 1970s when he wanted to buy a lot and build a home in a northern Peoria location. A White teacher at the same school was not turned down even though his financial resources did not match Hinton's. Fortunately, family support and spiritual values counterbalanced these and other negative experiences. Instead of bitterness, Hinton developed both aspects of compassion, a tender heart and a humanitarian's commitment to see that all children have what they need to develop to their fullest potential.

A Builder

Builders create from the ground up and also repair existing structures. Hinton has done both. His actions have guided the growth of the Valeska Hinton Center from a vision to reality and also transformed the program and environment at Harrison Primary School. Like a careful builder, Hinton does not waste any learnings. His first teachers were his parents, whose lessons he learned well. Diverted from his early ambition to become an architect, cast into a classroom crucible as an adult, he changed the chemistry through caring. Hinton has become a builder of people, schools, and community since that fateful first day of teaching in 1969 when the pull of caring relationships drew him into the profession.

In a nomination letter for a school district award, the president of the Children's Hospital Community Advisory Board wrote about Hinton, "I have served on a racial unity committee with Ken. I think he has done more for racial acceptance in the Peoria community than almost anyone I know. What a wonderful role model for our children!" Although Hinton has excelled at building bridges between the races, his caring for children is clearly not limited to children of color. In another nomination letter, Carla Montez, former president of the Parent Advisory Board, describes Hinton's love for children and how "he will go to herculean lengths to do what's best for the safety, well-being, and tending of our children." She also describes how his service extends beyond the grounds of the school. "Respected in the community, he is sought by many organizations . . . that look to Ken for his expertise, his good judgment, and his insights."

The following organizations are not a complete list of his activities, but illustrate the diversity of Hinton's community-building commitments: the African American Leadership Alliance, Boys and Girls Club of Peoria

Board, Enhanced Health/Community Health Team of the University of Illinois at Peoria School of Medicine, First of America Bank Board of Directors, Illinois State Board of Education's Advisory Group for Young Children, Mayor's Task Force on Youth, OSF Saint Francis Children's Hospital of Illinois Board, Peoria Area Chamber of Commerce Board, Peoria Area Community Foundation Advisory Board, Peoria Housing Advisory Board, Peoria Neighborhood Taskforce Committee, and the Southside Planning Taskforce. In 1997 he was a delegate to President Clinton's America's Promise Summit on Volunteerism. Hinton has received awards throughout his career that are also too numerous to list. Awards in the 1990s include the Dr. Martin Luther King Jr. Commemorative Service Leadership Award in 1993; the Illinois State Board of Education's "Those Who Excel" Award of Excellence in 1995; the Center for Prevention of Abuse "Partners in Peace Award," also in 1995; and, from the Peoria Area Association of Educational Office Professionals, the "Administrator of the Year" Award in 1997. Hinton was inducted into Peoria's African American Hall of Fame in 1994.

Nonconforming even as a child, Kenneth H. Hinton has become an educational leader who is a flexible innovator. His openness to learning has brought him many opportunities. From my perspective, the uncommon caring he offers others is partly a legacy from his family and partly a compensatory response to personal confrontations with discrimination. Nonconforming and compassionate, Hinton has a builder's eye. He has used his carpentry skills to build one house, his mother's last home before her death in 1996. He helped construct the home after her Southtown property was bought out by the city in the late 1980s. A builder's eye contributes to Hinton's ability to develop people and community. He sees what is needed. A builder works from an idea to a design, understands the importance of a strong foundation, makes adjustments, and knows that finishing work requires time and attention to details. Hinton instinctively follows these craft principles as he grows people and community from the ground up, from the inside out.

QUESTIONS FOR PERSONAL REFLECTION

In what ways do my own experiences as a student affect my work as an educator?

What dispositions from my family do I carry into my work as an educator?

What dispositions from my community and racial/ethnic identity do I carry into my work as an educator?

What patterns of mind, heart, and action create my silhouette?

⟞ 3 ⟝

A Family-Centered School

The way schools care about children is reflected in the way schools care
about the children's families. . . . There are many reasons for developing
school, family, and community partnerships. . . . However, the main reason
to create such partnerships is to help all youngsters succeed in school and
in later life. When parents, teachers, students, and others view one another
as partners in education, a caring community forms around students and
begins its work.

      —Joyce L. Epstein, "School/Family/Community Partnerships"

THE VALESKA HINTON Early Childhood Education Center was designed primarily to serve economically disadvantaged children and their families.
In November 1990, a group of Peoria educators and concerned citizens came
together as an advisory committee to contribute their ideas to the development of an early childhood school for children age three to six. They
wanted to find a way to coordinate services to young children, particularly
those from low-income families. Although programs such as Head Start
and other public and private programs served many children, many more
were falling through the cracks, putting them at greater risk for problems
with school.

    Five Southtown schools had been closed during the overlapping pro-
cesses of school integration and urban renewal. The neighborhood had been
promised replacements. This promise of new schools, the recognized need
for greater coordination of early childhood services, and a superintendent's
vision were the catalysts bringing together the original advisory group. The
superintendent who had the vision for a model early childhood center was
Dr. John Strand, who, shortly after the school opened, left the district to
become a consultant with the Efficacy Institute in Boston. In addition to
Hinton, appointed director/principal in November 1992, the other two
members of the leadership team who implemented and further developed
the school envisioned by the advisory committee were Dr. Judy Harris
Helm, Professional Development Coordinator from 1992 to 1996, who still

serves as a consultant to the school, and Sandra Burke, appointed Family
and Community Liaison Coordinator in 1992. Helm and Burke were both
members of the original advisory committee, but Hinton was not. The purpose of this chapter is to establish the professional context for Hinton's caring leadership by describing the school's program for children and their
families.

A SCHOOL FOR CHILDREN

The advisory committee of 15, chaired by Strand, met for two years,
reviewed many models and much research, debated curriculum recommendations and design, and developed a vision of a family-centered school
and "prototype community process to provide the best start for all its young,
urban children" (Helm, 1993b, p. 57). Many of the process ideas were
Strand's. When Hinton, Burke, and Helm were appointed by the group to
be the leadership team, the advisory committee also added 45 members,
evolving into a 60-person Task Force composed of community and school
district persons. The Task Force divided into six different working groups,
each focused on a different aspect of the planning. Building on the vision of
the advisory committee, in approximately seven months of intensive work
the groups further researched their areas and created detailed plans that
embodied the nine goals, listed below, previously developed by the advisory committee. This process was overseen by Hinton, with Burke and Helm
taking responsibility for chairing the groups. The six Task Force working
groups were Curriculum, School Climate and Organization, Staffing and
Professional Development, Student Assessment and Program Evaluation,
Student Selection, and Working with Families. Consultants worked with
these groups to present best practices research, and the decisions made by
the working groups broke many paradigms for public schools.

Philosophy

The original advisory committee developed the nine specific goals that
served as the foundation for all the planning of the Task Force groups:

1. Children will develop to their fullest potential in all areas.
2. Children will develop the ability to deal effectively with their environment becoming as able as possible in all areas.
3. Children will learn how to learn.
4. Children will learn to stay on task and persevere.
5. Children will learn to be actively engaged in the learning process.

6. Children will learn to take risks in learning.
7. Children will develop self-confidence and an appropriate level of independent decision-making.
8. Children will develop a knowledgeable, confident self-identity.
9. Children will develop comfortable, empathetic interactions with all people.

Whether these goals would be served became the standard against which all decisions about the school were made.

Before the school opened, Hinton asked Burke to write a statement of philosophy for the school. The statement went through several drafts until all persons involved had the opportunity to contribute ideas and wording to the final version. The philosophy became the focus of an opening-of-school ceremony through which the staff annually rededicates itself to the vision. The candle-lighting ceremony features a leadership candle, candles for each of the school's villages, and candles for each member of the staff. When all the candles are lighted, each person joins in reading the philosophy:

> WE BELIEVE that the society we have tomorrow depends on how we nurture, educate and challenge our children today. The love, protection, wisdom and guidance we invest in our children today will return to us in productive, useful citizens of the future.

> WE PLEDGE to promote the principles of self-esteem, self-discipline and respect for others, their diverse backgrounds, cultures and family structures. We will devote our energies to building harmonious environments in our homes, schools and communities.

> WE COMMIT to reducing barriers that prevent the joining of re-sources in providing the most effective services to our youth, families and to the community. A focus on the whole child will guide our actions.

> WE ENCOURAGE families, citizens, community organizations, schools and government to work together to create a safe and positive environment for all children, to stimulate their love of learning and to inspire them to reach their full potential.

Organizational Structure

The Task Force contributed to every element of the building's design and program. The leadership team, the villages, and the professional develop-ment school concept were organizational components designed to break paradigms for public schools. The evolution of these components illustrates how real forces shape even an ideal school.

Leadership Team. The advisory committee selected Hinton as principal because of his previous success as a principal with enhancing learning of economically disadvantaged students, working in partnership with parents, and creating a caring environment. The "director/principal" designation, instead of simply principal, emphasized that this was to be a school with collaborative leadership. From his appointment in November 1992 to the opening of the school on August 25, 1993, Hinton oversaw the completion and furnishing of the building, assuming responsibility for Task Force working group planning and overall school operations. Hinton traveled widely to sites around the country, educating himself about early childhood programs and facilities.

A member of the initial advisory committee and a former Bradley University early childhood education professor, Helm played a facilitative role during planning, furnishing the Task Force with research that led to many of the school's design concepts. "Although these concepts have appeared separately in schools, no early childhood programs to date have combined all of these concepts into a high impact design like this one," Helm wrote in an unpublished history of the project (1993a, p. 6). During her three years as Professional Development Coordinator, Helm provided initial orientation and ongoing training for all faculty on the curriculum, the project approach, the work sampling assessment system, and teaming. She was actively involved in selecting the original teachers and continued to play a key role in teacher selection. Hinton's and Helm's high standards prodded teachers to continue their own learning and professional development. In an analysis of the school's implication for society, Hinton has been called the "spiritual leader of the school community," and Helm "the motivator . . . the interpreter of practice" (Ward, 1996, p. 147). Helm left the center in the spring of 1996 to be available as a consultant to assist other school districts in building model early childhood programs similar to the Valeska Hinton Center program. The Professional Development Coordinator position remained unfilled until January 1999, but Helm continued in a consultant role during that time to provide staff development sessions for the teachers. Some of the position's other responsibilities were assumed by the lead teacher and by Hinton.

Burke, Family and Community Liaison Coordinator, has been responsible for development of the center's parent involvement model. Burke, a member of the original Task Force, has a master's in community agency counseling, and came to the project from the Tri-County Peoria Urban

League, where for six years she had directed programs comprising the agency's counseling services component. Her previous experience included a variety of leadership roles with early childhood education providers, including Head Start, and with PARC (Peoria Association for Retarded Citizens). Burke coordinates the student selection process, the parent outreach and educational programs, the parent support team programs, and sibling and extended care. The program for families has exceeded the vision of the original planning group. Burke feels strongly that all schools need a person in her position who can see things from a different perspective and help teachers work effectively with parents. "We need more people in our schools to fulfill this type of role and provide the supportive network so that all the other things that the school wants to do are enhanced," she explained.

Villages. The concepts of classrooms organized by villages, multiage classrooms, and looping were developed by the advisory committee. Each child is assigned to one of the four villages, remaining in the same village until ready for second grade at a neighborhood school. All children from a family are in the same village throughout their stay at the center. Teachers also remain with a village, work together, and get to know the families well, thus providing the continuity that Noddings (1995) advocates: "If we are concerned with caring and community, then we must make it possible for students and teachers to stay together for several years so that mutual trust can develop and students can feel a sense of belonging in their 'school-home'" (p. 679). A teacher and an associate teacher always staff each preprimary classroom, although this staffing pattern is subject to fluctuations in funding at the primary level. The children are part of a class for two years, staying with one teacher at the preprimary and another teacher at the primary level.

Preprimary classes meet four days a week, with Friday available to the teachers for home visits, planning, and staff development. Kindergarten students attend 4½ days, with Friday afternoon available for planning and staff development. First graders attend the full five days from 8:30 to 3:15 P.M. The teaching teams within a village plan cooperatively for large learning projects. The Red, Blue, and Yellow villages have three preprimary (multiage 3- and 4-year-olds) classes and two primary (multiage 5- and 6-year-olds) classrooms. Two of these preprimary classrooms are Head Start–funded rooms. The Green Village has only four classrooms because the Family Health Center, the first school-based health center in the district, occupies one of its classroom spaces. The Family Health Center is operated in conjunction with Methodist Medical Center of Illinois in collaboration with the University of Illinois College of Medicine.

Professional Development School. The goal of the proposed professional development component designed by the Task Force was replication, with "parallel early childhood units of pre kindergarten through second grade" (Helm, 1993a, p. 5) in each of the district's primary schools. Task Force members envisioned all prekindergarten through second grade teachers in the district spending a ten-week internship at the center. This aspect of the Task Force's plan and vision for the school has not materialized due to cost and a shift in the district's priorities. Nevertheless, the center still functions as a professional development hub for the district. College and university classes are offered at the center, and the building is used by the district for professional development programs on a wide range of topics. Hinton, Burke, and the faculty are active in the district's early childhood network, which meets monthly for professional development. Curriculum and teaching practices developed at the center are being disseminated through this kind of outreach rather than through teachers from other schools interning at the center. A professional development committee plans a whole year of activities based on a needs assessment, and all workshops for early childhood teachers are open to teachers from across the district.

Curriculum

The curriculum was largely unwritten in any conventional sense when the school opened, but its goals were clear. The overall goal of the curriculum is to have all children leave the center able to do second grade work in their neighborhood schools. The goals included in each domain of the Work Sampling System functioned initially as a curriculum. These seven domains are personal and social development, language and literacy, mathematical thinking, scientific thinking, social studies, the arts, and physical development. The written curriculum presents alternative strategies and resources for reaching the overall goal and the domain goals. The curriculum also is coordinated and tied in with district and state learning goals. Teaming in villages developed quickly during the first year as teachers worked together to meet the needs of the children and, with Helm's guidance, to learn and implement the work sampling system and project approach. Finally completed by 1996, the written curriculum was edited by Helm, assisted by lead teacher Sallee Beneke, and developed with significant faculty input through a committee process. This process included review by other early childhood teachers in the district, administrators, and parents.

Premises. Four premises underlie the curriculum and its goals. The first of these premises is, "Young children learn best through active, engaged, meaningful learning" (Helm & Beneke, 1996, p. 1), a premise supported for years by early childhood educators. Helm and Beneke explain that insights from recent brain research suggest that "learning is related to children's feelings and emotions, thus potentially influencing the important dispositions to learn. . . . that learning is interconnected and not isolated or compartmentalized into subject areas" (1996, p. 3). A rich variety of materials in the classroom environment facilitates active hands-on learning and construction of knowledge by the children. Verbalization is encouraged and attention given to the whole child, including social, emotional, physical, and academic development.

A second premise is, "Young children learn best when the school develops a sense of community for all participants" (Helm & Beneke, 1996, p. 4). This premise recognizes that children themselves will contribute to making their classroom community function well, but also acknowledges the power of partnership with parents to enhance students' learning.

The third premise is, "Young children function best in programs which value and reinforce continuity" (Helm & Beneke, 1996, p. 5). The village organization, staffing patterns, and classroom schedule foster continuity of personnel and provide large blocks of time so children can do complex, integrated in-depth study. About one-third of the day is allowed for child-initiated activities, according to the *Valeska Hinton Early Childhood Education Center Parent Handbook* (1998), which let the children experiment with active learning through constructive play that involves all their senses. Children are carefully transitioned from one classroom level to another, and all special services are delivered in the classroom.

Finally, the fourth premise is, "Young children learn best in environments which are appropriate for their age and stage of development and when they are with teachers who consider and respond to them as individuals" (Helm & Beneke, 1996, p. 7). Each classroom is divided into attractive learning centers, and furnishings are child-size. The small areas minimize distractions and allow the children to concentrate on what they are doing. Classrooms also have a central open area for activities involving the whole class. There is space to display children's work and also access to outdoor covered patios for another type of learning environment. Teachers are selected not only for their skills and credentials but because they care about young children and their families.

Project Approach. The project approach to learning is the major instructional strategy for accomplishing the goals of the curriculum. The overall aim of the project approach is "to cultivate the life of the young child's mind" (Katz & Chard, 1993, p. 3). The term *mind* is used to include "not only knowledge and skills, but also emotional, moral, and aesthetic sensibilities" (Katz &

Chard, 1993, p. 3). As explained by Helm, Beneke, and Steinheimer (1998), "The project approach is a good example of developmentally appropriate, active, engaging and meaningful learning" (p. 3). The children learn skills and build conceptual understanding by doing a guided in-depth study over time of a high-interest topic. Teachers and students design projects to find answers to students' questions. The project approach is similar to thematic teaching in potentially integrating content from a wide variety of areas, but differs from thematic teaching in focusing on the investigation and problem-solving work of the children. Figure 3.1 shows Hinton observing with interest as teachers Valerie Timmes and Judy Cagle talk with Dr. Helm about the student constructions that grew out of a real estate project completed by students in Cagle's classroom.

The project approach brings curriculum and teaching into closer alignment with what is known about children's development and learning. An important aspect of the project approach to learning is that the children become emotionally involved in this type of learning experience (Helm,

Figure 3.1. Hinton observes as, from left to right, teachers Valerie **Timmes** (kneeling) and Judy Cagle (standing) describe for Dr. Helm (sitting) a construction made by students as part of a real estate project. Photo by Jill Sanders-Goetz.

Beneke, & Steinheimer, 1998, p. 4). As explained by Greenspan, "Emotional reactions have often been thought to be secondary to cognitive perceptions, but in fact, in many circumstances they may be primary" (1997, p. 30). From studies with infants and children, he illustrates six developmental levels in the growth of the mind's deepest structural components: making sense of sensations; intimacy and relating; intentionality; purpose and inter-action; the level of images, ideas, and symbols; and finally the level of emo-tional thinking. Greenspan writes:

> After many months of monumental attainment, somewhere in the third or fourth year if all goes well, the six levels that constitute the foundation of an individual's mind should be solidly in place. . . . Though the issues faced in the later stages are different from those of the earliest years, emotional ties and relationships remain at the core of mental development. (1997, p. 103)

Assessment

The center's approach to assessment is multifaceted to allow for the diverse ways in which children learn and grow. The assessment processes are de-signed to give parents a comprehensive look at the progress of their chil-dren. Parents may do their own documenting of children's learning at home by developing a Family Portfolio, one of the options for parent involve-ment. At the Valeska Hinton Center, assessment enables educational plan-ning, program evaluation, and matching of curriculum to individual needs.

The primary instrument for keeping track of students' progress is the Work Sampling System developed at the University of Michigan (Meisels et al., 1994). This performance assessment is an alternative to group-administered, norm-referenced achievement tests for students in preschool through fifth grade. The system has "three complementary components: (1) developmental guidelines and checklists, (2) portfolios of children's work, and (3) summary reports completed by teachers" (Helm et al., 1998, p. 3). The Work Sampling System provides a flexible framework for assess-ment. Teachers make ongoing observations pertinent to growth using the Developmental Guidelines' checklists. For each item in the seven domains, teachers can identify the child's development on three levels: "Not Yet," "In Process," or "Proficient." The seven domains of learning on which the system is based are the curricular domains of personal and social devel-opment, language and literacy, mathematical thinking, scientific thinking, social studies, the arts, and physical development. Collection of materials for the students' portfolios also is a purposeful ongoing process that re-lates to the seven learning domains. The teacher continuously reviews the child's progress on the checklist and through the work collected in the portfolio; then, three times a year, the teacher writes a summary report that is shared with the parents.

Teachers also document children's learning in conjunction with class and village learning projects. Two other assessments are used. At the preprimary level a play assessment that evaluates social and emotional development is initiated when children are admitted to the center and reviewed as they progress through the preprimary program. At the primary level an additional checklist along with the summary reports keeps track of each child's reading and writing development.

Teacher Selection

Helm chaired the Task Force working group that devised the staff selection process, based on criteria developed by each working group. Each group designated the knowledge, skills, attitudes, and beliefs required for implementing the vision in their area of planning. Research about teachers successful with poor and minority children was also considered (Haberman, 1995). Unless time deadlines are too pressing, this process, used to select the original faculty, is still used to select teachers and associate teachers. Prospective teachers and associate teachers who inquire about positions at the center receive a letter describing the staff selection process, the philosophy statement, and background information about the center. They are required to submit designated portfolio items.

The first portfolio requirement is a résumé with an attached one-page summary highlighting how the individual's background meets the needs of the center. Applicants with teaching experience submit a diagram of their present classroom layout, designating where different activities occur. Inexperienced applicants submit a diagram of how they might set up a classroom. Each applicant also writes three typed half-page essays. Essay and portfolio items are graded by staff teams. Typical of the three essay items are the following questions: (1) What should be the relationship between teachers and parents and what role should parents play in the education of children? (2) How involved should a school be in the life of the child and family? (3) If you could pick the children to be in your classroom this year, what criteria would you use? Describe what your class might look like.

Top-scoring applicants are then invited to a 2-hour on-site selection process. The first event on site is the video analysis exercise, which provides an assessment of the candidate's ability to observe and evaluate children and teaching. A workbasket simulation tests level of skill in responding to real tasks. A reading team evaluates each candidate's anonymous written materials. The final part of the process is a face-to-face interview with a team of 5 to 10 persons composed of center staff, parents, and members of the school community. In all parts of the process, each candidate is evaluated based on fit with the mission and goals of the center. The point system is unsatisfactory (0 points), satisfactory (3 points), or highly satisfactory (5 points). In addition, the face-to-face interviewers listen for "fatal flaws," statements or behaviors that are "contradictory to the mission and goals of the center and should eliminate the candidate from continuing in the selection process." An example of such a statement was one interviewee's comment that "Children in the inner city can't learn as well as kids from the suburbs."

The interview is purposefully intimidating in order to simulate pressures the teachers might encounter teaching in a high-visibility pilot program. The process finds people who are committed to the students and able to interact positively with children and families, whatever their class or race. The quality of caring plus skill, persistence, and high expectations that will make children successful are what the selection process in its entirety is designed to evaluate, explained Hinton. When positions are offered to candidates who have scored well in the process, the candidates have experienced much success. "The validity of the process has become clear to me when lower-scoring candidates hired anyway have experienced challenges here," observed Hinton.

Student Selection

The Elementary and Secondary Education Act's Title I is the federal government's largest K–12 program to provide funding to schools with high numbers of low-income families. Title I originated as part of the Elementary and Secondary Education Act of 1965. The Valeska Hinton Center program, partially funded through Title I, actively recruits students from sections of the community served by the seven primary schools designated as Title I attendance areas. Enrollment at the Valeska Hinton Center is open, however, to families throughout the school district. One of the goals of the Task Force was as follows: "All students in low income areas of the city will reach a level of development by age 7 to meet expectations of the academic program for Grade 2 and onwards in the entire community." The student selection process facilitates enrollment of all 3- and 4-year-olds in a preschool program even if they are not selected to attend the Valeska Hinton Center. The process still in use is the one developed by the Student Selection working group of the Task Force. Student selection is Burke's responsibility. Screenings are still advertised widely, particularly in the target population areas, but the reputation of the school attracts parent inquiries from across the community throughout the year. School staff complete an enrollment questionnaire and follow up on each inquiry about the school. A letter and screening signup information are mailed in February to all parents who have inquired about enrollment.

The selection process occurs from March through May, with a new academic year beginning in late July. The school district works in conjunction with Head Start and other community agencies to locate and screen all 3- and 4-year-old children eligible for Title I services. Over 200 children are screened yearly. Figure 3.2 shows Family and Community Liaison Coordinator Sandra Burke participating in a meeting with representatives of the other early childhood programs.

Staff doing the screening use the Battelle Developmental Inventory (BDI) Screening Test in combination with a multiple-factor approach that combines biological and environmental data from teacher observations and the child's social history. The BDI Screening Test is a nationally standardized, individually administered assessment that covers developmental

Figure 3.2. Family and Community Liaison Coordinator Sandra Burke chairs a networking meeting of representatives from other early childhood programs in Peoria. Photo by Duane Zehr.

skills from birth to age 8 in the following five domains: personal-social, adaptive, motor, communication, and cognitive. If students have comparable educational needs according to the BDI Screening Test, the students selected first for the center will be those with other multiple risk factors. Staff log all the risk factors on a tracking spreadsheet as students are screened. Criteria points are totaled and recorded on the form. Other criteria involved in the process of selecting students and balancing the enrollment are the student's family attendance area and economic need, racial balance in the center, and racial balance in the sending schools plus impact on their enrollments in grades two through four. From the pool of eligible students, staff choose a cross-section of 100 3-year-olds for the early childhood center. Students with siblings already attending the center are given preference. The students not selected are encouraged to enroll in other early childhood programs in the Title I attendance areas: the STAR program (state of Illinois grant-funded pre-K at-risk program), Title I Preschool Program, Head Start Program, Evenstart Program, and early childhood programs offered by other community agencies.

During the 1995–96 academic year, when I completed my initial research the school was serving 375 of Peoria's young children. Although the goal is an equal racial balance, the enrollment was 39% Caucasian, 59% African American, 1% Hispanic, and 1% Asian. The gender balance was 50% female and 50% male, with 75% of the children from low-income families.

A SCHOOL FOR FAMILIES

A design concept generated by the original advisory committee was that "the school will function as a family center with GED Adult Basic Education classes, and parenting classes provided on site or through referral, networking and collaborative agreements with other agencies" (Helm, 1993a, p. 6). Through the leadership of Sandra Burke, Family and Community Liaison Coordinator, educational opportunities offered to parents at the center have exceeded that vision. A second design concept from the advisory committee was that "parents will be integral participants in the planning and operation of the school" (Helm, 1993a, p. 7). Hinton and Burke have worked together with the Parent Advisory Board to make this a reality. Finally, a variety of village and all-school social events further bond families with the center staff and with each other. Hinton and Burke clearly understand that the school and teachers must include parents as equal partners, an understanding many educators neither have nor practice. The center is joining the growing numbers of schools that are redefining parent involvement.

Philosophy

Nationally, Joyce Epstein has emerged as a primary spokesperson for the school/family/community partnership movement. She describes how challenges of partnership have created "an interdisciplinary field of inquiry into school, family, and community partnerships with 'caring' as a core concept" (1995, p. 701). Epstein writes:

> Research results . . . indicate that caring communities can be built, on purpose; that they include families that might not become involved on their own; and that, by their own reports, just about all families, students, and teachers believe that partnerships are important for helping students succeed across the grades. (1995, pp. 703–704)

Davies (1991) identifies three themes common to the newly emerging definition of "what has usually been called 'parent involvement'" (p. 377). These themes are: "Providing success for all children. . . . Serving the whole child. . . . Sharing responsibility" (p. 377). Davies concludes, however, that "these concepts are still radical in most urban schools" (p. 381). Burke describes the Valeska Hinton Center model of parent involvement as a strengths, empowerment, and prevention model. "At the center we think of families as diverse rather than at risk," Burke explained. The principles of the program are a starting point for program ideas and enable conflict resolution.

An official statement of *Principles of Family Support* was adopted by the Valeska Hinton Center Parent Advisory Board in November 1995. The lengthy statement of beliefs, adapted from the position of the Family Resources Coalition, includes commitment to a basic relationship between program and family of equality and respect. The principles commit to the importance of parents serving as resources and support for each other, and to recognition that seeking support and information is a sign of family strength. The principles commit the school to participation of all parents in core activities and educational programs, to family participation in program decisions, to serving as a bridge between families and other resources in the community, and to parent and school partnering in promoting the success of each child (*Valeska Hinton Early Childhood Education Center Parent Handbook*, 1998). The statement of principles reflects the trends and redefinition of parent involvement, still radical but being tested in pioneering schools like the Valeska Hinton Center across the country (Davies, 1991; Crowson, 1994; Epstein, 1995).

Organizational Structure

With Hinton responsible for overall school operations, functions of the family support staff are coordinated by Burke. When the school opened its doors Burke had no budget or staff, only a clear charge to create a model program for family involvement. Burke has developed the omnibus family outreach and support program, cultivated a wide range of partnerships, and also generated most of the grant funds that keep the programs going, a total of approximately $100,000 for the 1997–98 academic year. She has pulled in services from a variety of community agencies. In 1998, in-kind contributions from the many community partners have a dollar value greater than the actual dollars that fund the program.

Burke's Family Support Team in 1997–98 included a home school facilitator, family education teacher, parent educator, two parent library coordinators, a family support associate for each of the four villages, a prevention specialist from the community's Human Service Center staff, counselors, a secretary, and the sibling and extended care staff. Personnel are jointly funded by the school district and a combination of grants. Some personnel are contributed by collaborating agencies. A referral process to support children and families in crisis activates the Interdisciplinary Family Consultation Team, a group that meets weekly to facilitate family success through coordination of services to children and families in need of specialized help. Burke also works closely with the members of the Parent Advisory Board, composed of representatives from each village, that meets regularly and contributes to policy, planning, and other decision-making.

Burke is a skilled collaborator who is committed to the vision and principles of partnership with parents. From her perspective, the unique level of collaboration differentiates the Valeska Hinton Center from many other schools where collaboration is talked about but compartmentalization is practiced. "We truly collaborate and share funds, resources, and time across the different funding sources," Burke explained. "By being creative and overcoming territoriality, much more can be done with the same resources. Knowing the resources available in the community and the willingness to work with other agencies are also critical."

Program Opportunities, Services, and Activities

A full description of the program for families offered by the center is beyond the scope of this book. The following overview indicates the complexity and breadth of the program. Participating families sign a contract to be partners in their children's education by regularly volunteering in the classrooms, creating a vision statement for each child, and participating in center activities. The contract requires 36 activities per family per year in order to continue enrollment of a child for the following year. Participation is tracked through stamps on a card. The card helps parents make participation a priority, facilitates communication with teachers, and keeps staff alert to circumstances that signal a family's need for additional support. Turning in the completed cards to Burke is a moment of pride for parents. Notes and information from Hinton and Burke go out to families once a week in the mail bags that all students take home on Thursdays. The village newsletters and the *Hinton News* also go home in the mail bags. Parents can send notes and questions to the teachers when children bring their mail bags back to school on Mondays. A Parent Activity Calendar is published annually.

Parents receive a wide variety of educational opportunities, including formal GED and college classes as well as more informal nutrition, first aid, and parenting classes, to name only a few. Parents help to coordinate two annual conferences on parenting and leadership issues that are held on Saturdays at the center. All parents are invited to participate in an array of family social events. Some events, such as family potlucks and family game nights, are organized by villages. Whole-school events have included picnics, bus trips to see holiday light displays, Hinton Hop family dance nights, bowling, and even shopping expeditions by bus.

Services to parents are extensive. Sibling care during the school day is provided at no charge so that parents may conveniently volunteer in the classrooms and take advantage of educational opportunities. Child care is always available at no charge for evening events. Working parents enjoy the convenience of extended care for a small fee before and after school, as well as during Intersessions. The on-site Family Health Center provides medical care to children and their families through a fully equipped clinic staffed by doctors and nurse practitioners in cooperation with Methodist Medical Center.

Evolution of the Program

Burke's initial responsibility was to create the parent involvement model. Five years into the program, she is also focused on helping other schools replicate the model. "The big prize in all of this time and effort is if we can replicate this model to other schools so that other families can benefit," she explained. Burke and her staff have learned to give families many options. Flexibility is a key to working successfully with diverse families. An unexpected development has been awareness of the large numbers of grandparents raising grandchildren. For these families, particularly, the parent involvement contract for 36 participation credits may be waived, and staff are encouraged to support the grandparents any way they can. Aspects of the program that have exceeded the original vision include the Family Health Center and the Interdisciplinary Family Consultation Team. Burke's role with the district's early childhood network will continue to grow as more schools implement strategies for parental involvement. She will train all child care workers and family support associates as they are hired at other schools, for example.

Burke wrote the grant that provides the district's first licensed birth-to-3 child care center and a whole new layer of family support. Under way in August 1998 was a pilot program at the center for up to 30 children, ages birth to 3. The welfare-to-work initiative provided the incentive for this program, plus the realization that many young children were being brought to the center during the day by parents enrolled in GED classes and involved in volunteering, Burke explained. "Given what we now know about the important development occurring in the first three years of life, we wanted to serve these children," she elaborated. Some of the grant money will support hiring of two developmental case managers and increasing the four family support associate positions to full time. Valeska Hinton Center families with children under 3 years of age will have access to this case management support.

Outcomes

One of the new paradigms at the Valeska Hinton Center is that "Schools are for families, not just for children. School is a place where everyone goes to learn" (Montez, 1996, p. 10). A teacher expressed the same idea when she said, "This school is people/parent-friendly, really more of an educational center, not a school. Everyone walks away from here having learned something." The University of Illinois Center for Prevention Research and Development (1997) began survey research with Valeska Hinton parents in 1994–95 confirming this widespread learning. A sampling of 1996–97 responses from 313 parents indicates that the school is fulfilling its vision of being an educational center for families. Survey responses also indicate that parent satisfaction is related to staff and faculty attitudes.

Table 3.1 displays percentages of parents who report positive impacts from attending workshops and classes. Directions to the 313 parents were to check all items that applied. Even the three items with the lowest percentages indicate significant learning and growth, with 37% of the parents reporting going to the library more often, 24% reporting having enrolled in an education program, and 11% reporting having enrolled in a job training program.

Table 3.1. Impacts of Attending Workshops/Classes on Valeska Hinton Center Parents

Impact	*Percent* [a]
1. I read to my child more often	76
2. I will play an active role in my child's education	74
3. I encourage my child more often	73
4. I am more confident in my role as my child's most important teacher	72
5. I spend more time playing with/talking to my child	69
6. I am more responsive to my children's needs	68
7. I am learning new ideas about child-raising	68
8. I feel better about myself as a parent	63
9. My attitudes toward school and parent-school partnerships have improved	60
10. I better understand how my child grows and develops	58
11. My expectations for my child are more age-appropriate	53
12. I go to the library more often	37
13. I have enrolled in an education program	24
14. I have enrolled in a job training program	11

Source: Reprinted from *Valeska Hinton Center Technical Evaluation Report* (Center for Prevention Research and Development, University of Illinois, Urbana). Reproduced with permission.
[a]$N = 313$ parents.

Other results of the comprehensive survey were largely positive. The top barrier to school involvement was "Working during school hours," selected by 68% of the respondents. Only 1% of 313 parents cited any of the following as attitudinal barriers to involvement: "Do not feel welcomed by principal," "School staff are not friendly," and "Cultural differences." No parents indicated that "Racial differences" were barriers to school involvement. The only negative comments in response to an open-ended question concerned the difficulty of the required 36 participation credits for employed parents. According to Burke, however, 99% of the parents complete the requirement, and some parents even do more. As a whole, the survey responses indicate that parents are benefiting from the programs of the Valeska Hinton Center, a family-centered school.

The caring of the people who facilitate the program, not the program's structure and events, create this level of parent comfort, satisfaction, and learning. In explaining why some schools are not successful in building these partnerships with parents, Hinton faults attitudes, saying:

> Many teachers don't realize that children have something to offer, parents have something to offer them. It's almost like we who work in schools dictate the way the world is as opposed to knowing that we come with deficits too, or with holes, or with wants. . . . Teachers need to realize that we don't have all the answers and that teaching is a very personal and very humane thing. . . . It's also a very human

type of interaction that takes place between the teacher and child and parent. I want them to be aware of it and realize that everyone brings something to the table.

That the Valeska Hinton Center environment is colored by care shows consistently in the parents' responses to the University of Illinois survey. Parents are treated well by all school staff and are valued as important contributors to their children's learning. Their feelings and perspectives are respected. School personnel in other school settings might have perceived many of these low-income parents as not caring about their children. Highlighting this common misperception, Annatucci writes:

> I often heard Anglo teachers in villages complain that parents don't care about their children. Nothing could have been further from the truth, yet these teachers could not see how care was manifested. They complained that parents didn't make their children come to school, yet parents believed so strongly in the necessity of respecting children's thinking that they would say that if a child did not want to come to school, then the school must not be a place that welcomed the child. . . . Her story puts forth a truly revolutionary criterion for excellent and caring schools. The best schools are those that children care to attend. (1996, p. 33)

Children care to attend schools when Ken Hinton is their principal; so do their parents and family members. Central to his success has been bringing families into partnership with the school.

WHAT'S IN A NAME?

The Peoria Board of Education named the Valeska Hinton Early Childhood Education Center for a person who was a member of Hinton's extended family, a woman he always called "Auntie." Valeska Hinton was a prominent African American community activist. At the time of her death in 1991 she was eulogized as "the mother of the Peoria civil rights movement." She served from 1963 to 1968 as the first executive director of the Peoria Human Relations Commission before moving to the Chicago office of the United States Commission on Civil Rights. She was responsible for a seven-state area during her 14 years with that office. During her years in Peoria, Valeska Hinton was a catalyst for many opportunities that opened to African Americans. An editorial at the time of her death attempted to describe her:

> She has the intellect of a scientist, the insights of a philosopher, the sting of a satirist, the ambition of a politician, the courage of a soldier, the wit of everybody's favorite college professor, the compassion of a mother and the energy of all of them put together. ("Valeska," 1991, p. A4)

She is credited with bringing together the most powerful people in the community and changing the way they looked at race. The school named after her is also serving as a catalyst, transforming lives and the neighborhood. The school has already anchored the rebuilding of the Southtown neighborhood physically, as parks, residential, and commercial development have followed its 1993 opening. The school is also anchoring the neighborhood spiritually. It is a place where families from the neighborhood and the larger community are getting to know each other and to take responsibility for each other's children. Finally, the school has the potential, yet unfulfilled, to transform early childhood and primary education in the Peoria public schools.

The following excerpt from a newspaper article written two months before the school opened quotes newly appointed Director/Principal Hinton's vision for his work at the Valeska Hinton Early Childhood Education Center:

> "Parents' attitudes will change. Children will want to come to school. When the children are between 4 and 20 years old, we will see academic improvements," Hinton said. "Fewer will drop out of high school. More will go on to college. More will work, and fewer will be on welfare. Marriages will be more stable. This will be a powerful building. It's state-of-the-art—a school of the 21st century."
>
> Hinton has been widely acknowledged as the most capable person to lead the new center, yet even his karma seems tied to the place.
>
> Standing at the front door Wednesday morning looking north, Hinton points to a razed section of Southtown where he lived as a child. The ground he played on in his youth is now the turf where he will leave his professional mark as an educator with a vision to improve the lives of children and their families. (Howard, 1993, p. A3)

What's in a name? Belief in a better future, personal confidence, ability to inspire, persistence in the service of causes and people, leadership grounded in passionate caring, a lasting legacy—if the place is Peoria and the name is Hinton.

QUESTIONS FOR PERSONAL REFLECTION

What vision do I have for schools and my career as an educator?

How knowledgeable am I about community resources that support families?

What are my beliefs about the relationship between family involvement and student learning?

Do I have skills of collaboration?

ᕷ 4 ᕲ

Describing a Caring Environment

Compassion was one characteristic that captured our attention as we studied our schools over the past four years. Just walking onto some campuses
or entering some classrooms, we could feel the warmth and concern staff
had for each other and for their students. Parents, teachers, and administrators described their schools as families. . . . In short, our schools made
great strides in overcoming their bureaucratic pasts to become more human
organizations.

—Steve Ryan and Diane Friedlaender, "Becoming Caring: Changing
Relationships to Create Responsive Schools"

ONE DEFINITION OF school climate is as a "perceived environmental quality;
that set of factors that give the organisation a personality, a spirit, a milieu,
and atmosphere" (Dellar, 1997, p. 2). At the Valeska Hinton Center, the open
central courtyard and hallways with colorful red, blue, green, and yellow
tile pathways, the classrooms clustered in villages, the many rooms that
support the learning and family partnership, the layout of the building,
the tone and role of the Reception Office, and finally Hinton's personal
office all play a role in supporting the uniquely caring environment. However, having explored these features of the physical setting, one has only
described the underpinnings of the caring environment, only glimpsed its
energy, personality, spirit, milieu, and atmosphere. More important than
the building are the people. All persons at the school have worked deliberately to create the caring environment. For example, on an early visit to
the school I studied large handwritten charts about physical, social, and
emotional environment posted on the wall of a central hallway. The charts
listed desired descriptors for these three components of environment. In-
quiring, I learned that faculty had developed these descriptors through
a group process guided by Helm, during the time she was Professional
Development Coordinator. These charts are evidence that the caring
environment of the center has emerged as a result of leadership, delib-

erative planning, and staff involvement. This chapter opens with a descriptive exploration of the physical environment of the school. Presentation of the results of my research on faculty, staff, and parents' perceptions of the environment establishes that the school environment is caring. Following two veteran teachers' comparisons of the environments of the schools for which Hinton has served as the principal, the chapter concludes with an interpretation of the school logo.

EXPLORING THE PHYSICAL ENVIRONMENT

It is not the building that creates the special environment of the Valeska Hinton Center, although many people comment initially on the attractiveness of the contemporary 63,000-square-foot, single-story facility. Hinton is quick to say about the caring environment, "We could do this in any building." Underpinning the caring environment of any school, however, are aspects of the physical environment, including the design of the building. Having participated as a member of the community Task Force, a local architect worked diligently to transfer the vision of the planners into a physical reality, a place where all people, adults as well as children, could be comfortable. The Task Force members envisioned a warm, welcoming, and positive school space that would bring families into the educational process as partners. Built for $7 million, the facility provides children with an ideal setting for a best practices early childhood education.

The spacious lawn areas that surround the school are well-landscaped green spaces planted with a variety of young trees. A local nursery, one of the center's Adopt-a-School partners, has contributed planning and planting, but the custodians and students care for the special areas, like the prairie grasses and butterfly gardens. Figure 4.1 is a view of the north side of the building at midafternoon with adults leading children from the Blue Village to their waiting buses.

Central Foyer

Persons entering the building from either the north or south doors walk into a spacious open circular central foyer with natural lighting coming from a large skylight. Staff keep the area seasonally decorated from floor to ceiling with large festive flags always hanging under the skylight. In July, when the new school year begins, these flags are welcome banners, but the messages and colors of the banners change with the seasons. I've seen the foyer filled with mums and pumpkins for fall, a winter holiday tree and greenery in December, and planters overflowing with spring flowers. For several weeks one spring a large table featured a habitat for six rapidly

Figure 4.1. From left to right, student teacher Angela Bromley and associate teachers Laura Bankert and Betty Kniss lead children from the Blue Village to their waiting buses at the end of the school day. Photo by Duane Zehr.

growing baby ducks. Another time, as a culmination of a village project, the foyer was a bake shop with children as shopkeepers dispensing treats. In the entry hall on the more frequently used south side of the building is a large well-stocked aquarium with a nearby bench that welcomes visitors to sit down and relax. The other decorations in the school halls are displays of children's work on the walls, documentation carefully arranged by teachers with labels and photographs. These frequently changing displays of individual and group projects tell the dynamic story of how learning at the center happens. The walls are a warm ivory, and the floor features a mosaic design of colored tiles that extends down the hallways, with yellow and green pathways going in one direction and red and blue in the other. These pathways make it possible for even the youngest children coming into the central foyer to find the way to their villages.

Classroom Villages

The classrooms cluster into four villages, with the Yellow and Green villages on the east end of the building and the Red and Blue villages at the west end, each village having its own adjoining outdoor play area. Each village play area has sidewalks for riding toys, large colorful pieces of play equipment, sand areas, and even a covered patio that makes outdoor activities possible even when the weather is not perfect. Classrooms are large and subdivided into cozy learning nooks for individuals and small groups. A carpeted meeting area in the center of each classroom is for large group gatherings. Teachers serve the students breakfast, lunch, and snacks family-style in their classrooms, so the building has a central kitchen where meals are prepared but not a conventional cafeteria. The village plan recognizes the African American folk wisdom of the school's motto: "It takes a whole village to raise a child." Colorful accents for each village wing are the appropriate primary color and serve to further identify a child's home area. Each village contains four or five classrooms, a large planning office with desks for each teacher, a smaller room for planning or conferencing, and a village kitchen.

When teachers and students in a village collaborate on a learning project, the resulting constructions often occupy all the village's hallways. Once the Blue Village turned its hallways into a remarkable reconstruction of a hospital. The children had visited a hospital and each group had been responsible for bringing back a drawing of a different area. With creative building materials, the children accurately recreated a reception area, an elevator, a patient room with a bed, a gift shop, the nursery, a skeleton, and even an X-ray machine that was made out of a large moving box. The patient room included a cleverly adjustable bed with patient tray, a remote control for the TV, a get-well card, a water pitcher, and an IV bag on a realistic tall stand. The children proudly and eagerly gave me a tour of their hospital.

Program Support and Meeting Rooms

Opening directly off the central foyer are the Reception Office, Activity Room, Family Support Team Office, and Parent-Teacher Resource Library. Near these rooms, but opening off side hallways, are the Sibling Care Room, Learning Library, Parent Meeting Room, Community Meeting Room, and Staff Meeting Room. A brief description of these rooms, organized by purpose, completes the physical exploration.

Several rooms primarily support the needs of families and staff. The Family Support Team Office houses the Home–School Facilitator and the Family Support Associates assigned to each village. These staff cultivate and nurture links between the families and the school. Filled with professional development materials and a large work area for teachers, the Parent-Teacher Resource Library also serves parents. The library loans reading, play, and art materials for parents to take home and use with their children.

Located off a side hallway, selected graduates of the on-site Child Development Associate program staff a Sibling Care Room for the convenience of parents volunteering in a classroom or conferring with a teacher. Babies can sleep, and the other young children enjoy activities and trained, competent care. The Parent Meeting Room was the site of the evening meeting described in the opening pages of the book. It is welcoming and comfortable, like a living room, and available for parents who want to just relax. The room is also used for a variety of meetings. An inspiring quote always heads the information on a message board next to the Parent Meeting Room. For example, one day the sign read, "A confident child is usually successful in life." These messages add to the school's positive environment for parents and staff and contribute to learning. The Community Meeting Room has a traditional meeting area with chairs and tables, but also includes a kitchen and a conversation area of comfortable sofas and chairs. The GED classes meet here, as well as other parent activities.

Several other rooms primarily support teacher and student activities. The Activity Room is a large multipurpose room that has been used for everything from active indoor play, to meetings, to a production by a visiting ballet company. Throughout the week, classroom groups visit the Learning Library, a large multimedia art, drama, and computer room. There is a recessed stage for plays and story time, as well as a castle for fantasy play. This room also houses the before- and after-school extended care programs available for children of working parents. Finally, the Staff Meeting Room is furnished with comfortable professional office chairs and moveable tables such as would be found in a corporate environment. When the staff meets the furniture arrangement is usually circular, but the room is often arranged theater-style for professional development activities and classes.

All the offices and rooms surrounding the open central courtyard have windows instead of solid walls on their inside edges, making people and their working spaces visible. These window walls contribute to links among the staff and help create the openness to which parents and visitors respond. Sitting in the office in the morning, one can watch through the windows as the children come into the building and turn down one hall or the other, following the colored pathways in search of their villages.

One day I watched a teacher comfort a small girl who walked in from the buses in tears. She stooped down and said to the child, "You're Ebony, aren't you?" Then she noticed the girl's brother standing off with his friends, and motioned to him. "You're Ebony's brother, aren't you? I've been hearing good things about you. Why don't you be a good big brother and walk your sister to her classroom?" said the teacher. The boy responded by putting his arm around his sister protectively and asking her why she was crying. After she settled her sobs, he walked down the hall with her. I saw countless examples of this kind of caring and teaching of caring as adults paid attention to children's emotions, knew the children and could call them by name, and encouraged the children to help and care for each other.

Reception Office

The "Reception Office" sign above the door reinforces that visiting persons are to be "received," and no one left ungreeted or just standing. Just as the structure of the villages facilitates small family-like clusters for the children, the central location of the Reception Office, staffed by two full-time secretaries, facilitates weblike connections and leadership from the center. Colors in the office are soft blues, greens, and grays. The school by design has no faculty lounge. Faculty tend to come into the office in the morning to check their mailboxes and just visit. In twos or threes, faculty also will sit in the comfortable reception area chairs after school and just talk. As one teacher put it, "There is no other office like this. It feels comfortable. You can chit-chat. It's not off-limits. We are told up front usually that the office is a place for business, not to socialize, but here it is different."

The carpeted office is always seasonally decorated, and the secretaries are equally welcoming to everyone, large or small, old or young. The office looks lived in, like a home, but is well-organized and clean in spite of the constant traffic. One secretary works behind a long, wide, soft blue counter, and the other has an angled desk work area in the corner next to the door to Hinton's personal office. A huge teddy bear sits in one of the several comfortable chairs lining the wall of windows that allow for looking out into the central foyer. One morning I watched an angry child pick up that bear, hug it fiercely, and then throw it on the ground. The huggable bear facilitated an expression of anger that hurt no one. Feeling better, the child picked up the bear and sat down beside it in the chair. The office bear can be both therapy and a playmate for a waiting child.

Hinton's Office

Hinton's office door opens off the Reception Office. The office is spacious, with a conference table, comfortable chairs, a large desk, and even a small bed that is often a resting spot for a child not feeling well or needing time out of the classroom. A child's drawing is usually taped to the front of the desk. A large stuffed brown bear and an equally large panda occupy two of the chairs. Teachers are in and out of the office continually, as are children. Along the wall behind Hinton's desk is a large ledge on which rest numerous awards that Hinton and the school have received and a collection of pictures of the school and children. On a side wall is a large poster of the school logo and a window that looks out toward the north side of the school. The desk faces a long wall on which hang two inspirational posters, one about "attitude" and the other about "goals." In between the posters is a framed article about the school. In a corner a bright colorful quilt covers a small rocking chair that sits next to a wagon. There are materials everywhere, and the office conveys a sense that much is happening. Hinton typically sits at the conference table to meet with adults, but gets down on one knee to talk with visiting or misbehaving children. Not once did I see Hinton sit behind his desk to talk with anyone. Although he does take phone calls sitting at his desk, he is just as often on the phone in the Reception Office.

PERCEPTIONS OF THE SCHOOL'S ENVIRONMENT

Educators and researchers view school environment from a variety of perspectives. A frequent synonym for environment is *climate*, which Sergiovanni defines as "a form of organizational *energy* whose telling effects on the school depend upon how this energy is channeled and directed" (1991, p. 215). Sergiovanni's analysis of climate lists seven descriptors that appear recurrently in writings about organizational climate (p. 215). One of the seven is "warmth and support," defined as "the feeling that friendliness is a valued norm in the organization, that members trust one another and offer support to one another. The feeling that good relationships prevail in the work environment" (p. 216). This descriptor is of something similar to caring, although the word *caring* is not used explicitly. Creators of inventories designed to assess or measure organizational climate invariably consider caring an aspect of climate. For example, caring shows up in the phrase "warmth and support" on one such instrument (Kolb, Rubin, & McIntyre, 1984, p. 343). Hoy, Tarter, and Kottkamp's Organizational Health Inventory for secondary schools (1991) includes caring in the definition of the principal behavior called "consideration." A newly developed School Organisational Climate Questionnaire, appropriate for secondary schools, contains a category called "peer cohesion," defined as "the extent to which teachers are friendly towards and supportive of one another" (Dellar, 1997, p. 3).

Culture is another word associated with discussions of school environment. Whereas climate and culture are similar, Sergiovanni captures their differences, writing:

> Climate is concerned with the process and style of a school's organizational life rather than its content and substance. School culture, by contrast, is more

normative than school climate in the sense that it is a reflection of the shared values, beliefs, and commitments of school members across an array of dimensions that include but extend beyond interpersonal life. (1991, p. 218)

Caring is clearly a component of both climate and culture. Caring influences climate through relationships and influences culture as a value or norm. The perception and reality of caring can be assessed as an aspect of the environment of any school.

Before understanding and analyzing the components of Hinton's caring leadership, I needed to establish that the Valeska Hinton Center was indeed a caring school environment. Although in the community both the school and principal had a reputation for caring, my interview questions sought to confirm this. Hinton introduced me to the staff at a faculty meeting after school in early September 1995, simply telling the staff I was from Bradley University and that I was going to be studying the environment of the school. I thanked them for welcoming me into their school and explained that I would be making interview appointments. Neither Hinton nor I mentioned caring.

Research Procedures

Perceptions of the environment presented in this chapter were developed from on-site interviewing and data collection over a 6-month period. Data analysis was ongoing during that time, with emerging themes generated through inductive content analysis of observation field notes, interview notes and transcripts, and school documents. From September 1995 through February 1996, I can account for a total of 88 hours of specific activities at the Valeska Hinton Center. Included in that total are 5 hours in private conversations with Hinton, 9 hours in parent meetings, 19 hours observing in the office, and 10 hours observing a variety of other meetings and activities. I spent a minimum of 1 day a week at the school. The secretaries placed copies of all information that went to staff and parents in an office mail box designated as mine. These materials included the principal's weekly staff bulletins, parent newsletters, and other information about special events or deadlines.

Demographics of the 1995–96 staff were obtained from their responses to a written survey. Reluctant to describe the staff with racial labels and divisions, I decided to see how staff members themselves would answer the question "How do you describe your race/ethnicity?" They answered as follows: African American, 9; Black, 8; Hispanic, 1; American, 2; Caucasian, 12; human, 1; White, 23; WASP, 1; and Irish American Indian, 1; 2 people put a question mark in the space and 1 person left it blank. Of the

61 full-time staff members, 5 were male and 56 female. In terms of age, the staff was composed of 15 persons in their 20s, 14 in their 30s, 22 in their 40s, 9 in their 50s and one person in her 60s.

The 1995–96 staff consisted of a professional development coordinator, a family and community liaison coordinator, 2 secretaries, a lead teacher, 19 classroom teachers, 2 special education resource teachers, an art/learning center teacher, a speech pathologist, 14 teacher associates, a family educator, a home school facilitator, 7 family support personnel serving in various roles, 3 custodians, 5 food service personnel, a nurse practitioner, and a health center clerk. Teaching experience of the 19 classroom teachers ranged from 1 to 28 years, with 10 teachers having less than 5 years of experience, 5 teachers whose experience falls in the 6- to 20-year category, and 4 teachers in the 21- to 28-year category. Of the staff members, 45 (73.77%) were parents, and 9 of these had children attending the school.

I spent approximately 45 hours interviewing staff and parents. In scheduled half-hour interviews, all 61 full-time staff members answered the same three questions. The first question was, "Please explain your role and length of time in that role here at the Valeska Hinton Center." The second question was, "If you could only use one word to describe the environment of the Valeska Hinton Center, what would that one word be?" Follow-up questions to the latter were: "Could you tell me more about what you mean by that?" and "In what ways does the principal contribute to creating this environment?" If the person chose the word *caring*, the interview ended after the follow-up questions. If the person did not choose *caring* as the word, he or she was then asked the third question: "Is 'caring' also a word that would describe the environment of the Valeska Hinton Center?" A total of 40 parents, distributed equally among the four villages, were also asked the same questions about the school environment and the principal's contributions to it. These parents were interviewed either as they were coming into or leaving the building on regular school days, or at the series of classroom-by-classroom parent meetings held by the principal in January and February. Some of the interviews were as brief as 10 minutes. Others lasted as long as 45 minutes.

Results and Interpretation

The following discussion and interpretation organizes the words offered in response to the primary interview question by categories that emerged through analysis: caring, affective descriptors, program-focused descriptors, evaluative descriptors, and uniqueness descriptors. Interview responses indicated that clearly, for both staff and parents, the caring aspects of the school's environment loom large.

Caring. Eight staff members interviewed chose the word *caring* as their single-word descriptor of the school environment. All 53 staff persons who did not initially choose *caring* answered that *caring* was another word that described the school environment, and provided illustrations in response to the follow-up question, "In what ways does the principal contribute to a caring environment?" The initial word choice of 5 parents was *caring*. With 1 exception, all the parents whose initial word choice had not been *caring*, or a total of 34 parents, agreed that *caring* was also a word that described the environment of the center. The exception was a parent whose child had just been returned to her custody from the Illinois Department of Child and Family Services. Her first response was, "It depends. You have to mind your p's and q's." She quickly added that from her own experience, particularly with Mr. Hinton, she would have to say yes, the environment was caring. Of the 101 persons interviewed, a total of 13 (12.87%) chose *caring* as the best single word descriptor of the school environment. As one person put it, "Everyone in the center cares about the children and their families as well as each other, and you see it in what they do."

Affective Descriptors. Words related to caring or expressive of the affective dimension of the environment constituted a large category of responses. For staff, these caring-related words were: *family,* chosen by 6 people; *nurturing, love,* and *warm,* each chosen by 2 people; and single word choices of the words *secure, stability,* and *welcoming.* For parents, other caring-related words were *loving,* chosen by 2 parents; and single word choices of *lovability, concerned, family, nurturing,* and *warm.* Noted in further conversation by many persons interviewed were feelings of welcome and warmth, an involvement of all staff in caring about and valuing the children and their families, as well as each other. Several persons mentioned in elaborating on their responses that the environment is about more than caring, that the appropriate word is love.

At the end of a lengthy interview, I asked Hinton what one word he would choose to describe the environment. He answered, "I see our institution as in evolution, and I guess that the one word I would choose is *nurturing.*" He elaborated on the importance to him of an environment that nurtures the growth and development toward wholeness of all persons on the staff so that each will be able to pass that nurturing along to the children and their families.

A range of other single word choices reflects the affective dimension of the school environment. These choices are italicized in sentences I've created to capture this aspect of the environment: The environment is *energetic, invigorating,* and *enthusiastic* as staff involve themselves in caring for one another, the children, and their families; staff *commitment* creates an *involved motivated* environment for students and parents; the school offers students a *comfortable, friendly, happy,* and *peaceful* environment, which is *encouraging* and *uplifting.*

In the words of one of the secretaries,

> It's *hope* that we get here that we don't get anywhere else. We know we can do better, that we can uplift the families and the children. There is nothing we can't achieve because of so much hope, inspiration, positive energy that is contagious for everyone who steps in here.

Said one family support person, "Everything is always so positive. I was real impressed the first day and week how everyone smiled and spoke to you, how everyone was always willing to do things, and it carried through the whole year." In summary, a teacher explained her choice of the word *dedicated* with, "The vision is so deeply embedded in all of us."

Program-Focused Descriptors. One category of words included program-focused descriptors. *Busy* was chosen by three persons, one of whom said "It's always hopping at the Hinton!" *Challenging* was chosen twice. Other words each chosen by one staff person were: *collaborative, diverse, educational, child-focused, family-oriented, open, teacher-friendly,* and *teaming.* Words each chosen by one parent were: *challenging, enriching, family-oriented, individualized, open,* and *rewarding.* Many staff members spoke of a commitment to deliver a quality program that meets all the children's needs—physical, academic, social, and emotional. A committed staff delivers the educational program in spite of obstacles, such as a lack of full funding that periodically affects staffing. The commitment to the mission of serving children and the full range of their developmental needs is real, and neither that commitment nor caring stop when the children leave to go home.

Evaluative Descriptors. In another category were words that provided overall quality or evaluative descriptors of the program. *Awesome* and *wonderful* were each chosen by 3 staff persons, with *exciting* chosen by 2. In this category, other words chosen by 1 person each included *fantastic, fascinating, good,* and *great.* A word chosen by 7 parents was *excellent,* with *great* chosen by 3. In this category, other words, each chosen by 1 parent, included: *beautiful, fantastic, magnificent, stupendous,* and *wonderful.* One enthusiastic staff member called the school "the perfect place for young kids to start off." A secretary elaborated her choice of *awesome* by saying,

This is truly the way I feel every school should be, where everyone is part of a team—children, faculty, parents, and community. When we care for mom and dad, too, and build their skills and knowledge, make them part of their children's education, help them want to do better, then we are going to be able to turn things around.

Interestingly, the largest category of responses for parents were those overall quality descriptor words such as *excellent*. In elaborating on their choices, parents typically connected the quality of the program with the caring environment. For example, one parent said, "It's like the family that children need when they are away from their parents. It's great!" Another parent said, "It's like taking my child to a relative's house. I don't have to worry about him. They take care of everything here." Parents repeatedly praised teachers. One parent said, "Teachers here teach from their hearts, not for the pay. You can tell they really love to teach." Finally, several parents mentioned the growth they had observed in their children, that they were learning socially as well as academically. "Children learn faster here, and it's not just the equipment," said a parent.

Uniqueness Descriptors. One final category of words offered to describe the center focused on its being nontraditional. These words were: *different, innovative,* its *own little world,* and *unique.* As a teacher associate explained, "We are always trying different teaching techniques because we feel this will help the children learn better." The teacher who said the center was its own little world explained that she meant inclusive or comprehensive. She elaborated that she found the school hard to describe. "It's a place where we deal with everything—teachers, teacher development, students, students' development, parents, parent development. It's not just for children. Sometimes I forget it is just a school, because so much happens here." Another staff member chose *unique,* she said, because "there are very few schools that exist today that provide young children opportunity to develop in areas of social, physical, emotional, and academic skills."

Words Chosen by Both Staff and Parents. Of particular importance to a description of the caring environment of the Valeska Hinton Center are the 10 words spontaneously selected by both staff and parents. Important because they were chosen by *both* staff and parents, these 10 words are extremely significant to my conclusion that the environment of the Valeska Hinton Center is caring. Numerically, these words account for the choices of 46 persons (45.54%) of the 101 interviewed. I use these 10 italicized words in the following sentences to create a summary description of the uniquely caring environment of the school:

The school is fundamentally *caring*. It is like an ideal *family*, both *warm* and *nurturing*, offering *love* in a variety of ways to all who enter. The school is *wonderful*, *great*, and a *fantastic* place, offering a program that is *challenging*—a nontraditional *unique* school.

COMPARING CARING SCHOOLS

In initial interviews in 1995–96, five persons commented on Hinton's contributions to the caring environment at Harrison as well as at the Valeska Hinton Center. In March 1997, I went back to two of these teachers, pictured in Figure 3.1, for in-depth interviews. Whereas an assumption might be that the Valeska Hinton Center is the epitome of a caring school environment, these teachers who also taught at Harrison Primary School believe Harrison's caring environment to have been equally engulfing. Primarily serving students from a public housing project, Harrison's low-income enrollment is consistently at 99%. Judy Cagle, a veteran of 20-plus years of teaching, said she thought Hinton's caring leadership made even more of a difference at Harrison because the needs there were so acute, that the caring naturally evolved out of the depths of the problems. Valerie Timmes, also a veteran of 20-plus years of teaching, believes the new staff of the Valeska Hinton Center has done well in 3 years to create a warm caring environment, but that it does not compare yet with Harrison.

A K–8 school of 1,100 students in the 1950s and 1960s, Harrison changed and problems developed as the racial composition of residents of the Harrison Homes changed. Situated on the edge of a public housing project, "the Harrison student body's commonality was such that we had a whole school of children with enormous needs," said Cagle, continuing that "the programs that evolved under Hinton's leadership were in response to those needs." A local reporter's story portrays one needy child's success at Harrison:

> When Lopez Robinson celebrated his 7th birthday last August, he had the verbal skills of a 4-year-old, and could barely read.
>
> As is the case for many children at Harrison School, all the ingredients for causing academic failure were present in Lopez' life. Born into poverty, he is the offspring of an unemployed single parent with four other children to raise.
>
> But what Lopez had going for him was an experimental class with 14 other children who were judged at risk of failing first grade. He's had teachers who gave him large doses of attention, affection, and real life experiences, and a mother willing to listen and follow up when he came home carrying books.

In six months Lopez' language development has leap-frogged three years.

He reads. He expresses himself. He asks questions. He describes things. . . . Principal Ken Hinton calls it "adaptive instruction," which means teachers adapt their teaching strategies to the learning styles of children, with a heavy emphasis on sensory learning, self-esteem and attitude adjustment. (Bailey, 1989, p. A1)

Caring led to new programs like this special First Graders At Risk classroom, with staff and Hinton thinking up the programs during focused brainstorming sessions. Teachers and all other school staff members were invited to these sessions. Some happened at Hinton's home on Friday evenings, while others took place at school. The first program developed was the First Graders At Risk program. Subsequent programs included Health Fairs, Parenting for Success, Growing Together, and a Developmental Kindergarten, an idea that originated with Cagle and another teacher. When the school became the first in the district to adopt the computer-based Writing to Read curriculum, three teachers and Hinton went to Atlanta for special IBM training. All of these innovative programs, and others as well, were developed and implemented in response to students' needs during a 2- to 3-year period.

As a new principal, Hinton was successful in promoting the learning of students at Harrison Primary School by working with teachers to develop programs that responded to the students' needs and by drawing in parents. Some of these programs were featured in a news story headlined "Illiteracy Loses Turf in the Projects":

Language development in a first grade transition class . . . has improved one to three years across the board since last fall. Comprehension has increased dramatically in a second grade class . . . thanks to a cooperative learning program devised by the teacher and a University of Illinois professor, Hinton said. He said the program has students actively involved in reading and teaching one another.

There's a discovery room where students can see and feel things that before were misunderstood words in textbooks. Frequent field trips—to the Illinois Air National Guard base, a play at the Civic Center, the mall, a restaurant—take students to places they have never been before.

Harrison has the only computer Writing to Read program in District 150. A resource library for parents is on the drawing board. Scaffolding obstructs the hallways where murals are being painted of characters from storybook fables. Motivational messages abound, from The Little Train That Could to an I Want To Be wall that has children forecasting their professions. . . . The children are responding, as are the parents, Hinton said. . . . "All of this came about because we knew our children had the ability. We knew they could do it, but they weren't doing it," Hinton said. "Educators have to realize it's not the child's attitude. It's the instructor's attitude (toward the children). If they start out believing they can, they will. Somebody believed in me." (Bailey, 1989, p. A14)

In addition to all the new programs, Hinton instituted serving breakfast at Harrison, the first school in the district to do so. One difference he immediately noticed was that fewer students were getting sick at lunch, as many had previously when they had not eaten since the day before. The response of students was so dramatic that at first teachers thought the children were getting too much sugar because they became so active, he recalled.

At Harrison, the successful transformation of the school first required letting go of the old and then implementing the new. "That transformation process built a unique shared history that Valeska Hinton Center faculty will not experience because the new center has simply evolved from a particular point in time," said Cagle. From her perspective, each process is different and has its own bondings and complexities. Hinton came to Harrison in his first administrative position as an Administrative Assistant, working with an also newly appointed principal over a period of several years to restore order. For example, Cagle said, "We made the school more presentable and cleaner. We spruced it up because a neglected physical setting is an indicator of a lack of caring." When the district restructured and created middle schools, Harrison became a K–4 school. Hinton was sent to a middle school as Administrative Assistant for one year before returning to Harrison as principal in 1987. Hinton recalls that even though most of the staff knew him from his years as Administrative Assistant, not everyone was thrilled with his appointment, because they were at the same time experiencing the loss of the former principal, who was transferred to a high school principalship. Hinton recalls playing music of KC and The Sunshine band at his first staff meeting and announcing, "Treat these children as if they were your own or mine." He said he soon got a call from the Central Office as well as comments from several teachers that he ought to "slow down, that some of the entrenched teachers were not ready for that message."

Cagle reminisced about Hinton's role in the transformation of the Harrison environment. Thinking about that time, she remembers Hinton having both caring and a toughness about him simultaneously as he led the faculty through the transformation process. The toughness was reflected in his high expectations for students' achievement and behaviors. For example, she described how Hinton began to establish himself as the principal. Room by room, he called each class to the gym and gave them the stern message that any inappropriate behavior would not be tolerated. On the other hand, she also remembered Hinton's doing little things to express appreciation for the staff, like the Mothers Day long-stemmed carnations he gave to all the women, "because we were all mothers to the children," he said. Cagle ended this second interview with an analogy. "Remembering Harrison," she said, "is like remembering early days from a marriage, being poor, struggling, and traveling unknown paths. We had to figure everything out based on the tremendous needs of the children and their families." Calling the Valeska Hinton Center a different experience, she said, "I think when the young teachers here think of caring schools they will probably all compare other schools with the Valeska Hinton Center, but I still use Harrison as a point of reference."

Whereas Cagle had been a teacher at Harrison even before Hinton came to the school, Valerie Timmes came to Harrison after the transformation led by Hinton was well under way. Timmes left a school considered more desirable as a place to teach to come to Harrison because she wanted to be in an urban school again, in an environment where she could make a real difference to children in need. She describes being overwhelmed by what she saw and the warm feeling she experienced when she observed at Harrison and went for an interview. She saw innovative teaching throughout the school, things that were not happening in other schools in the district, and decided she wanted to be a part of it, but was afraid she would not be good enough. She was amazed at how Hinton could call students by name and knew their families. "The kids came to him like a magnet," she said, and there was respect for the school in the neighborhood, with the gangs leaving the school and its grounds alone.

Timmes recalled her first parent open house with some chagrin. Whereas other teachers had 85% attendance, or almost everyone, she had only 15%, just five parents. "Hinton suggested that I do a home visit," she said, "and my whole life changed." She finally realized what was needed and has continued to grow from his constant support and encouragement of her professional development. She sees him as a principal who believes that students must have all the basic physiological and safety needs of Maslow's hierarchy met before learning can happen, and then he acts on that belief, finding for the children whatever they need—even food, shoes, and clothing. "Whereas other principals might have those thoughts," Timmes said, "he translates the thoughts into action." Even with all her years of teaching, Harrison was her first experience of a school where there was a vision and the expectation that teachers were professionals. She described the importance to her of the dedication ceremony held at the opening of each school year. The ceremony, built around a candle-lighting ritual, restates and recommits the staff to the school's vision for children and their families. Timmes said she also had not seen parent involvement and parent education programs at other schools in the district like those that had been developed at Harrison.

Timmes finds Hinton unequaled in his attention to research and his ability to get teachers to pay attention to the research about learning and teaching. "I went to my first professional conference when I was at Harrison, fifteen years into my career," she said, because Hinton told her about it and encouraged her to go. "Another thing Ken did at Harrison was put literature in our boxes for us to read. We would follow up with discussion at meetings. I never had experienced that before." At Harrison she began to speak out more against injustice, to be an advocate for what is right, and to stay current with professional reading.

Speaking about the evolution of caring at the Valeska Hinton Center, Timmes finds it to be coming along, but commented that Valeska Hinton Center teachers who visit Harrison still comment on its warmth. At Harrison, what she calls the "underdog phenomenon" of teaching at a school perceived by outsiders to be undesirable contributed to the connectedness. She experiences connections among the Valeska Hinton Center staff becoming closer each year. From her perspective, although the village structure is uniquely good for the children and families, to some degree it hampers building connections across villages among the staff. She said that Hinton is doing a variety of things to help create those connections, such as having juice and donuts available in the Parent Meeting Room on Friday mornings so that teachers can stop in and visit with each other. He has also set up a social committee. From her perspective, "the Valeska Hinton Center would not be like it is without Ken." She said that if he were to leave "the spirit or emotional rhythm of the place would leave with him," but he has instilled the vision in her to such a degree that she would want to stay to help it continue.

Speaking of the two schools, Hinton acknowledged that it was more difficult changing the environment at Harrison than building the caring environment at the Valeska Hinton Center. He explained,

> It took two or three years at Harrison, but finally the culture of the school was such that we understood why we were there. We were there for the children. At Harrison there were challenges to developing caring, with teachers in conflict with each other. I had to hold up the importance of adults working together positively, to work with developmental stages of the teachers. There were discipline, morale, and academic concerns.

"Here at the Valeska Hinton Center, methods can be subtle," Hinton explained. The process has been easier because "it's more about getting and keeping a feeling than transforming a whole culture." He continued, "In formation of this school we looked for people who had blatant or hidden qualities of caring, plus skill and persistence and the high expectations to make children successful." The process has not been without challenges, however. Hinton described how the superintendent hired three independent-thinking people (himself, Helm, and Burke) to be an administrative team, all with different ideas about how to proceed. "To keep this leadership team intact required diplomacy on my part," he commented. During the first year and much of the second, he consciously deferred to the others so that a model of cooperation developed as a pattern for the village teams. "It has been a slower trust-building process here," in Hinton's opinion, partly "because with no preformed groups, I couldn't work with any informal leadership." Cagle said that this fall she had "sensed a new environment emerging with Ken taking charge, making changes. With the shared leadership, his being respectful of the others, sometimes it has been difficult to get answers. I now know that he will make the decisions. This is much more comfortable for me."

THE SCHOOL LOGO

The logo (Figure 4.2) of the Valeska Hinton Early Childhood Education Center, developed by a volunteer as an expression of the energy, personality, and spirit of the school as a community, provides a memorable image of important elements of this caring school environment. One day in conversation, Hinton interpreted the logo for me. A number of designs were submitted, but this one was chosen partly because it had a folk or ethnic feeling, similar to African American fabric work. This particular design also was chosen because it was unusual, nontraditional like the school. The two hands reaching skyward represent the hands of all the people at the center—children, parents, and staff—who are all involved in reaching, growing, and changing. The stars symbolize how all the people involved with the center—children, parents, and staff—are stars in their own right as they reflect and shine in their own ways. The sun and moon are in the picture together because the center is always open, day or night, for people and programs. The solid rectangular line around the design represents that the Center provides a strong supportive system for growth, that a person isn't alone here but is included in a community of people who care about each other. And finally, the wavy lines of the edges of the piece of the sky are a reminder of the importance of flexibility.

Figure 4.2. Valeska Hinton Center logo.

QUESTIONS FOR PERSONAL REFLECTION

What one word would I use to describe the environment of my school or my child's school?

What one word would I use to describe the environment of a school I would want my own child to attend?

How do I contribute to creating a caring school environment?

⋘ 5 ⋙

Tough Decisions and a Typical Day

Do not be shy about your leadership role. Take responsibility and make decisions, but do so in a caring way. Realize the power that sharing leadership and decision making brings. Listen to others, build consensus, support success, and set a personal example by honoring the dignity of each individual in the schoolhouse.

—Harvey B. Alvy and Pam Robbins, *If I Only Knew . . .*
Success Strategies for Navigating the Principalship

THE FIRST FOUR CHAPTERS constitute the ground, in an artistic sense, for the portrait of Hinton. An artist uses the word *ground* to refer to the first coat of paint applied to a surface, or to the background of a painting against which the other parts of the work appear superimposed. The ground of this portrait in words is already multilayered, composed of theoretical, historical, personal, and professional contexts against which to view Hinton's leadership. Hinton's leadership has contributed to caring school environments at the middle, primary, and early childhood levels. His caring, flexible, and participative approach to decision-making has contributed to his success as a principal. In this chapter I provide a glimpse of Hinton in action to establish a foundation of trustworthiness for the six themes of his leadership, to be developed in Chapter 6.

One focus of my watching and listening in 1995–96 was Hinton's response to his perception that morale at the Valeska Hinton Center was low, a perception he shared during our first interview. How caring and flexibility affected his approach to rebuilding morale and making other tough decisions is documented in this chapter, and the complexity of infusing caring into decision-making is explored. Much of what I discovered about caring leadership through months of interviewing and observing lies embedded in my notes from the first full day I spent observing in the office, on September 12, 1995. A recounting of highlights of that typical day concludes the chapter.

FLEXIBLE DECISION-MAKING

When asked about his flexible approach to decision-making, Hinton replied, "There is great joy in reaching beyond what the rules say when the existence of another individual—child, parent, or teacher—is improved." Reading most principalship or introduction to educational administration textbooks, one finds few references to joy, reaching beyond the rules, or making caring decisions. More typical than the language of the Alvy and Robbins quotation that opens this chapter is the language of Ubben and Hughes (1997), for example, from their chapter on decisions: "Rational processes are required" (p. 29). The quote is from a chapter about settings for decisions, models of decision processing, and the work group as a problem-solving unit. Ubben and Hughes emphasize making decisions and solving problems at the proper level, with staff involvement when appropriate. Throughout the chapter the authors advocate using a rational decision-making process, whatever the type of decision, as the best way "to reach a sound judgment in a timely manner that will result in a solution that is in the best interests of all concerned" (Ubben & Hughes, 1997, p. 30).

A currently popular synonym for *decision-making* is *problem-solving*, the subject of research by Leithwood and Steinbach (1995). Part of their extensive research distinguishes between problem-solving processes used by expert and typical principals. They conclude that "relatively few differences between effective and typical principals' responses" (p. 65) exist when the problems are clear or structured, but substantial differences surface in responses to unclear or ill-structured problems. These differences include problem interpretation, goals for problem-solving, principles, constraints, solution processes, and affect (pp. 51–52).

Hinton's usual decision-making processes match with several of Leithwood and Steinbach's (1995) conclusions about expert principals. According to their research, expert principals collect much information, consider implications of decisions for students, use principles to make decisions, use consultation to get information, and project a calm, confident mood (pp. 51–52). Cognitive flexibility also emerges in the Leithwood and Steinbach research as a chief attribute of expert problem-solvers. However, because the evidence was correlational in nature, and from a small sample, they conclude that it offers "only weak support for the importance of such flexibility for principals' problem-solving. Further research is needed to understand fully the role that cognitive flexibility plays in expert administrative problem solving" (p. 215). Identifying mood, principles, and values as "the 'non-rational' elements of problem solving so severely neglected in previous research on administrator decision making" (p. 66), Leithwood and Steinbach conclude that these elements also warrant further study. In spite of recommending further study, they make a definitive statement about the role of values for expert principals: "Values are pervasive in the problem solving of educational administrators, explicitly so in the case of experts; this was among the most significant results of the research, in terms of our own learning" (p. 312).

As a new administrator, Hinton faced a tough decision about how to handle discipline. School norms and his personal values conflicted. Illegal now, at that time in Illinois and the Peoria public schools, spankings were legal and a norm. Hinton understood spanking to be the quickest way to remedy some situations. He observed that spanking was oddly effective with some children, but he always articulated his emotional connection with and care for any student he spanked. Over time Hinton observed some teachers spanking children without any emotional connection or regard for the children's psychological health and development. He believed this was doing damage to the children, which went against his fundamental principle of doing what is best for them. Hinton called a meeting and announced to the Harrison staff that he would no longer spank misbehaving students, that it took too much from his spirit. Understanding his example to mean that they should also refrain from spankings, many staff who had no other strategies were lost. After several faculty members came to him in frustration, he and they tackled misbehavior as a school community. The results of that collaboration contributed to the school's positive redirection.

How Hinton's approach to discipline evolved suggests his humanness, flexibility, and orientation toward values. Ultimately, he ignored the norms and interpreted the problem of discipline differently. He prefers, for example, to say to some of the students who misbehave, "Yes, you are ornery, but you are still loved. I know you're going to do those kinds of things, but it's going to pass. You're just going through a stage." He encourages faculty to see children not as the sum of their immediate actions, but as they will be when fully mature. Able to discipline and nurture simultaneously, he does not have a conventional approach to misbehavior. Hinton's approach is very positive and nurturing rather than negative and punitive. No matter what the age of the students, this approach has always gotten results.

RECOMMENDING NONRENEWAL

Handling discipline is just one example of the many bureaucratic responsibilities of a principal. Combining a caring attitude and ethic with bureaucratic responsibilities can be challenging because of caring's conflicting claims. Courtney and Noblit (1994) highlight the contradiction between the bureaucratic responsibilities inherent in the role of the principal and the commitment to persons evidenced when a principal cultivates personal relationships with staff:

> Developing connections with people is always so difficult, but more so when one has an official position and responsibility. Such a position communicates to others that at some point you may have to act in accordance with your responsibility to the possible detriment of other commitments and connections. In this way, an official position may undermine caring. (p. 71)

Hinton chooses to have more personal relationships, to be more involved with staff and students in terms of their personal well-being. A guiding principle for Hinton is, "We will do what is best for the children." His decision when principal at Harrison School to take away a veteran teacher's class illustrates a contradiction of caring as well as his principle of doing what is best for the children.

Hinton's work with a Harrison teacher to change some of her classroom practices had been ongoing. He was cautiously optimistic in the fall that she would be able to make the necessary changes. Several weeks into the semester, he determined that her teaching behaviors and burned-out attitude were still hurting the students psychologically. Given no evidence from her of willingness to change, he simply decided in mid-fall that she would hurt no more children. When approached by Hinton, the other three teachers at the same grade level agreed to take the children from her classroom. With her children divided among the other teachers, reassigned to tutorial work with students from other classes, the teacher decided it would be her last year. The approach illustrates that there is more than one way to recommend nonrenewal. Some might call taking away the teacher's students harsh rather than caring, but Hinton's action was clearly based on caring for the children. The contradiction illustrates the complexity of caring decision-making. Paradoxically, his action also can be viewed as demonstrating care for a teacher who had lost the heart to care by encouraging her to leave the profession.

Whenever Hinton addresses staff about instructional concerns, he is careful to be caring. He recognizes, however, that the need to supervise and evaluate staff creates the potential for harming any caring culture. When I arrived at the Valeska Hinton Center in September 1995 to begin my research, Hinton was facing morale consequences from a decision he had made the previous spring. He chose not to rehire a beginning probationary teacher knowing that the decision would cause third- and fourth-year teachers, as well as the associate teachers, to feel less safe and secure. He cared for the teacher, but his responsibility to care for the children had a higher claim, even though he knew the trust-building process under way among staff would suffer. Again, Hinton made a tough decision based on what he believed was best for the children. When we talked he said, "It has been six months and will take another six months to get back to where we were." Explaining his reasons for the decision, Hinton spoke of the value of caring:

> People who work here need to be emotionally secure and self-confident. That quality of being able to care for a student is important enough for me to release a teacher. Teachers have to display a level of care for children and their families and have expectations for the children. . . . If teachers do not care for whom they teach, then it is a technical experience. . . . When a teacher does not have this care for a child, it shows in their actions, remarks, even body language.

Having made this tough nonrenewal decision, Hinton expected that morale in the fall would not be the same as in the preceding year. Therefore, he was not surprised when this turned out to be true.

Rebuilding Morale

Two factors contributed to lowered faculty morale throughout the building in the fall of 1995. Closely following the release of the teacher in June, the new year began in late July without associate teachers in almost all classrooms. Central Office administrators had not filled the associate teacher positions due to funding uncertainties. Hinton's decision-making process in response to the reality of lowered staff morale illustrates the problem-solving of an expert principal. Lowered morale is an ill-structured problem, existing as it does in hearts, minds, and perceptions. Even though causes may be clear, how to respond is often unclear. Hinton followed his typical problem-solving processes, gathering a large amount of information in consultation with staff. His own mood was consistently calm and confident, and not at all defensive. He asked how people were feeling. Believing that if he didn't do something, the pressure would manifest in unacceptable ways, Hinton began the systematic process of talking with everyone about their concerns. No one in the building was left out of the process. At the same time, he lobbied Central Office to begin filling the positions as funds became available.

Hinton moved from his perception that teacher morale was lower than acceptable into a process of dialogue. The focus of each session was a question: "Where are we in terms of where we want to be?" I attended the meeting on September 19 with five people who work in the kitchen preparing meals. Hinton began by saying, "We are here for the children," and then complimented the staff on helping teachers serve the meals. Their replies expressed pleasure and interest when Hinton asked how they were feeling about what they did and how they saw things. Several shared concerns. Hinton asked for and received good suggestions about how to respond. Throughout the meeting he made written notes of each concern and suggestion. He invited them to attend faculty meetings if that would help with their work. Bringing the meeting to a close, he asked how they were treated by the other staff and if anything else was on their minds. Hinton concluded, "Please let me know if you can think of any ways that our school could be better, and let me know if you see anyone not being respectful and treating others with dignity." Summing up the spirit of the meeting, one of the people offered the perfect closure. "It starts with us," she said.

As a result of either individual conferences or meetings, Hinton had collected by October a list of approximately 225 items of concern to address. These were all neatly handwritten on a thick stack of single sheets of paper. He used the three-week October Intersession to analyze the concerns and ponder his choices. Hinton decided to address the most important issue for each group first. For teachers and associate teachers, the main concern definitely was the time consumed by their work. At a faculty meeting after the October Intersession Hinton shared with teachers and associate teachers what he had learned from them. He reemphasized the importance of treating everyone with equal respect. Making clear his understanding of the time pressure they were feeling, he said that he wanted each of them to leave by 4 P.M., and no more professional development meetings would be scheduled before or after school. He would be getting substitutes so that professional development activities could be held during school time. He articulated repeatedly that he cared about the staff, and understood that they were people with personal as well as professional lives. The final piece of good news he shared was his success in getting central office to fund the five associate teacher positions that remained unfilled. The persons would be hired within two weeks. The meeting and his immediate actions to relieve the time pressure marked a turning point for morale. He demonstrated understanding that their caring for the children was dependent upon feeling cared for and good about themselves, too. The entire process of his response to lowered morale demonstrates expert decision-making skills. His allowing me as an outsider to conduct research on caring at a time when he understood faculty morale to be low is remarkable, in retrospect, and displays the calm confidence of an expert principal.

STABILIZING THE PROGRAM

Feeling a need to stabilize the program, Hinton continued to discuss both the staffing and time issues with faculty. One alternative for alleviating the stress of beginning the year without a full staff was to eliminate first grade entirely. Enrollment history indicated that some parents were choosing to send their children to parochial or neighborhood schools beginning with first grade, so first grade numbers were lower than enrollment at any other level. The multiage K–1 primary classrooms were the most difficult for the teachers to handle without associate teachers. Following up on the first children from the center to enter second grade classrooms in their neighborhood schools, Hinton discovered that students' difficulties with transition and differences in performance were related to staffing. Those children who had been in the primary classrooms staffed the entire year by a teacher and associate teacher were performing well above average, while the children whose classrooms had been understaffed were not. After several weeks of dialogue with faculty and central office staff, Hinton's recommendation was that all first graders be sent to their neighborhood schools and that the center become a Pre-K school. Central office staff would commit to fully supporting the staff with associate teachers in every room, since this change would reduce the total number of teachers required. When Hinton met with the teachers on November 28 to get their final thoughts, they were in agreement with his recommendation.

The final step in his decision-making process was to take the proposal to the Parent Advisory Board. Hinton shared the recommendation to eliminate first grade with the Parent Advisory Board at a meeting on December 7. Dressed casually in slacks and a tan turtleneck shirt, Hinton stayed seated as he presented to the parents his proposal "to stabilize the program." The curriculum was meant to be delivered by a teacher and an associate teacher, he began, yet the school experienced recurring staffing problems at the beginning of each year. When teachers have to share the associate teachers there is disequity in the program, he explained, and we spend much time and energy compensating. He cautioned that funding for the five associate teachers just hired was not assured for the coming year. He concluded the presentation by saying that he had met with the teachers and their general feeling was that maybe a 3-year program would be better, but he needed the opinion of the parents before making a final decision.

The opening response from Advisory Board President Lisa Schlehuber set the tone. "Your best may not have been achieved, but it's way above the district's potential. I want to keep first grade." Much discussion of the funding structure and process ensued, with Hinton explaining how the allocation of Title I monies causes the district's budget to be uncertain until mid-October. Some parents expressed determination to do fund-raising if necessary to pay the associate teachers' salaries. Hinton suggested other alternatives, including different multiage groupings. A parent brought up the widespread hope that the school would enhance the educational system on a larger scale. "What will happen to that goal if first grade is lost?" he asked. At this point in the discussion, Hinton asked for comments from other parents who had not spoken. Many hands went up. Altogether, 35 persons were present, including 8 teachers.

After comments from an additional 8 persons, Hinton said, "I think I get the drift. We will keep first grade. We do have a Plan B, but we will need your support." He would go back to the staff, he said, and together they would devise a way to alter the program that would not water it down. He expected that their decision would be to have single-age rather than multiage classrooms at the primary level. The kindergarten classrooms would continue to have a teacher and an associate teacher, but the first grade teachers would start the year without associate teachers. Several teachers contributed to the discussion at this point. It really takes two teachers to make multiage classrooms work, they said. As the discussion concluded, Hinton urged the Advisory Board to focus on parent involvement rather than fund-raising. He called it a "sign of the times" that we need to alter the program to make it work, given the uncertainties of school funding in Illinois. "We will stabilize and insure the program," he assured the parents.

Curious, I asked Hinton later why he stayed seated at the table during the meeting, even when making his presentation, and why he had dressed so informally. Were those conscious decisions? He answered that he is always conscious of the politics of his relationship with the parents, the teachers' relationship with him, and his relationship with central administration. "I was a guest at the meeting, or a participant in the meeting, and I try to retain that profile," he explained. The outcome of this meeting and subsequent meetings with faculty was to adjust the program beginning in late January by separating the K–1 multiage classrooms into kindergarten and first grade rooms for the remainder of the school year. During the meeting with parents, Hinton reversed the proposal he and the faculty had developed. "What was professionally and what would have been personally easier would have been to do what we wanted to do, but that was not the parents' desire," he said. The decision to separate the classes immediately raised staff morale and gave first grade teachers the ability to work intensively with the children to ensure a smooth transition from the center to their neighborhood schools.

The faculty and Hinton continued to dialogue, renewed their commitment to multiage classrooms, and eventually agreed on a modified multiage format for the 1996–97 year. On the basis of the needs of particular children, the staff created one predominantly kindergarten classroom for 5-year-olds. The rest of the primary rooms were K–1 and included both 5- and 6-year-olds. The general pattern in 1997–98 was three multiage preprimary classrooms per village for 3- and 4-year-olds and two multiage primary rooms. The primary classrooms all contained both 5- and 6-year-old children, but certain rooms were predominantly for kindergartners or for first graders, depending again upon the needs of the students. The staff continues to build the primary classrooms according to the needs of the students and experimented with several multiage classrooms of 4- and 5-year-olds. Movement among the classrooms in a village, depending upon the individual learning needs of children, continues to occur and may happen at midyear. The reversal and subsequent revisiting of how best to stabilize the program illustrate Hinton's flexibility in action and his commitment to working with parents. The decision's process and outcomes demonstrate flexibility and the principle of "doing what is best for the children," even if that means confusion and more work for himself and the staff.

STRENGTHENING FAMILY INVOLVEMENT

Another tough decision made during the fall of 1995, at the urging of the Parent Advisory Board, was to strengthen the family participation requirement by stiffening the consequences for nonparticipation. Through a Pledge of Partnership, required parent participation had been a component of the program since the school opened. Most parents had honored their commitments, but some had not. Enhancing parent involvement was on the Parent Advisory Board agenda at its October 1995 meeting, which I attended. The charge from the administration to the parents was "to help develop a definition and determine what consequence, if any, should be attached to non-compliance." After a lengthy discussion, the board's position was established and recorded in the minutes:

> VHECEC's Family Involvement policy should focus on the growth and development of the child and family as defined by the Philosophy Statement for the Center. Criteria should include a Family Participation Plan developed at the time of acceptance into the Center. These plans should be made in conjunction with teachers and Family Support Associates. A method for implementation, improved monitoring and follow-up, and overall communication should be established. (Reeves, October 26, 1995)

During the next month Hinton and Burke met with the Executive Committee of the Parent Advisory Board to develop specific policy recommendations. At the November 30 meeting of the Parent Advisory Board, Burke presented for the board's review a statement of "Principles of Family Support." Parents made several suggestions in response, including that throughout the document the word "family" rather than "parent" consistently be used. Following the discussion, Burke presented a draft of a Family Involvement Contract to the Parent Advisory Board members for their reaction and comments. The final item of the draft contract stipulated that the person signing understood the consequences: "If my/our family involvement plan is not developed or my/our commitment is not fulfilled, my/our child and family will be asked to leave the Center, in order to provide an opportunity for another family," the contract language read. The contract had been drafted by the Executive Committee of the Parent Advisory Board, including the president, Burke, Hinton, and one representative from each village. Hinton reiterated that he and the school would do whatever the Parent Advisory Board recommended about family involvement. The decision made that night was the beginning of a strengthened policy. The Parent Advisory Board members decided that families not involved to the degree required would be asked to take their children out of the program. The policy would apply to preprimary children, but not those in the primary classes.

Even before this formal decision, a few children had been dropped because of family nonparticipation. Hinton had found these decisions difficult without any written guidelines. Now clear communication with families about this potential consequence of nonparticipation would occur from the beginning. "The charge the Advisory Board has given to Sandy and me is to address those parents who are not doing what they are supposed to be in terms of supporting their child's development by being here and doing certain things," Hinton explained. He estimated that the families of about 20 preprimary children would be contacted initially and given a month to make some changes. His experience has been that some will respond and some will not. The Parent Advisory Board suggested a trial period for the contract and that it be monitored, reviewed, and reaffirmed annually. Everyone left the meeting clear that the implementation of the policy would be individualized, with each family's particular situation evaluated and respected. Teachers would have the authority to make the final decision in the event of extenuating circumstances.

Although dropping children from the center is a difficult decision, Hinton explained why it is sometimes a necessary decision:

> It is going to have to be at the expense of some of the children, and that's the hard part, because most of the time the children who you have to eliminate are the children who need it the most. Once you

do that you have set a precedent and the people know if you go to this school that involvement is required. The public relations is ultimately positive even though it is a negative thing that you do. The parents who are part of the school go out in the community and reaffirm that you have to support your child's education if you go to the Valeska Hinton Center.

Hinton's comfort with the tough decision is that of a builder with the big picture or blueprint in mind. In this decision, the good of the school and its reputation are the priorities. Hinton and the staff believe that parent involvement is critical in the short and long term because parent involvement affects what students learn. If students are not learning as much as they might, then they and their families will not get maximum benefit from the program offered. "If students do not perform when they leave the center, then parents' perceptions of the quality of the school will diminish. It could become a neighborhood school and we would lose our ability to influence the entire school system," said Hinton. Asking some families to leave strengthens the whole program, ultimately benefiting the students who remain and those yet to come.

LEADERSHIP GROUNDED IN CARING

Ground is used as both a noun and a verb. As a noun, we use the word in a variety of expressions, including to gain or lose ground, to break new ground, to run something into the ground, to cut the ground out from under someone's feet, and common ground. As a verb, its most basic meaning is "to provide a basis or foundation for" (McLeod, 1987, p. 442). Hinton's foundational value of doing what is best for children shines through layers of complexity as the ground of each of the decisions elaborated in this chapter. The examples illustrate, however, that making decisions grounded in caring is not simple. The decision to discontinue spanking misbehaving children required reversal of a disciplinary pattern with which the faculty was comfortable. Hinton reached beyond precedent and the rules to care for children and work with the Harrison faculty to change a whole school's approach to discipline. The two nonrenewal decisions show how caring for children and caring for individual staff members may sometimes be incompatible. The decision at the Parent Advisory Board meeting to keep first grade at the center illustrates Hinton's underlying flexibility and willingness to respond to the wishes of the families. He continues to work with the faculty to develop appropriate grade configurations. He cares enough to make and remake decisions until the children's needs are met. The decision to require a harsh consequence for nonparticipation by parents will be flexibly enforced and again illustrates caring's contradictory claims. The parents on the Parent Advisory Board pushed for families not honoring their commitments to be asked to leave. The clash between what the Parent Advisory Board perceived as a just consequence and Hinton's care for the affected children illustrates that sometimes claims of justice and caring can conflict. Whereas some children will suffer a harsh consequence for their parents' irresponsibility, children in years to come will benefit from the school's taking parent involvement seriously. Bureaucratic responsibilities inherent in the principal's role contribute to the complexity. No easy formula exists for leadership or decision-making grounded in caring.

Sketch of a Typical Day

I began my study in early September by spending an entire day at the school, arriving at 6:45 A.M. to find Ken walking down the hall and some children already there. As previously described, Hinton's personal office opens off what is called the Reception Office, one of four main rooms opening off the central foyer. Much informal visiting happens in this office throughout the day, but particularly in the morning as teachers check their boxes and other staff arrive. Conversations and laughter about lesson plans and materials were common among the teachers.

This particular morning there were many questions about the new copy machine. Hinton closed his personal office door only twice the entire day, once for a 20-minute meeting with a secretary and once when he was meeting with someone about a confidential matter involving a social service agency and a family. He was just as likely to answer or talk with people on the phone in the Reception Office as in his personal office. This practice of his added to the feeling of everyone being an equal member of the team. Dressed in a short-sleeved shirt, slacks, and a tie, Hinton welcomed everyone who came into the office warmly and by name, including children. I counted at least a dozen children who sought out the principal to say hello or show him something and get a hug before Hinton left for a district meeting about 9:15 A.M. According to my notes, in the first two hours of the day Hinton had also interacted with 30 adults, in person and by phone, in his personal office and in the outer Reception Office.

Returning about 11:30 A.M. from the district meeting, Hinton talked with his secretary about the copy machine replacement, asked her to send flowers to a funeral, and, seeing a need, made a quick decision to take home the Russian-speaking grandmother and child who were having to wait because the "Door-to-Door" van was not coming as scheduled. Back in about a half-hour, he sat at the secretary's desk and made a call about getting something fixed in the air conditioning system. His next interaction was with a parent who dropped in because her son was not supposed to be having breakfast, but was being charged anyway. He said he would take care of it, and had done so before the day was over. He welcomed Dr. Lilian Katz, who had come to work with Dr. Helm; then, hearing a child crying, he said, "I'm going to go see who that is." Hinton followed the sound of the crying, and I followed him, to a preprimary classroom, where he went in, talked kindly with the child, hugged her, and said, "I can't do my work when I hear you crying. You take your nap now." He was back in the office in just a few minutes, where almost immediately a teacher confronted him, seeking his advice about a particular child. About an hour later another child came into his office, brought down by an associate teacher who reported that he had thrown pencils. Hinton, on the phone in his personal office, acknowledged the child by touching him on the shoulder, and let him just roam around the office. Finished with the phone conversation, Hinton asked the child to sit in the chair in front of his desk. On his knees, Hinton talked very quietly with the child while he retied his shoelaces. Then Hinton went on about his work, eventually telling the calmed-down child it was time for him to go back to class.

The rest of the afternoon was a stream of people, phone calls, and projects, including arrangements for a faculty meeting on teaming facilitated by lead teacher Sallee Beneke. Hinton spent time helping the nurse devise a system for filing the physicals. He answered the phone in the Reception Office and even made several photocopies. Either Hinton or secretaries Jackie Petty and Micheline Pascal welcomed and greeted by name everyone who came into the office. As school ended and the children went to the busses or were picked up by parents, another flurry of children came in and out of the office to tell "Mr. Hinton," as they call him, good-bye, show him their papers, and collect hugs and praise. I counted interactions with 25 children that day, mainly student-initiated. He greeted all these children by name and praised each one for something. Hinton clearly did not consider interactions with the children interruptions, whether they were eager children wanting their morning hugs or misbehaving children.

Hinton's attention moved easily from a conversation about a request to go to Chicago to attend the meeting of the Governor's Task Force on Early Childhood to a conversation with Micheline about diet soup and exercise. He laughed and promised himself to start exercise tomorrow, then filled the soda machines and talked with several parents. When both secretaries left at 4 P.M., Hinton began answering the phones in the Reception Office, talked with teachers as they left, and greeted persons coming for a prenatal class, one of several educational parent events scheduled for the late afternoon and evening. In the entire day I did not hear one negative thing said by anyone about any situation, child, person, or family. When I left at 4:45 P.M., my mind and notebook full, Ken Hinton was still there.

Although unusual, the Valeska Hinton Center is similar to thousands of schools across the country in at least the following ways: a majority of its students are children of poverty, many from changing and challenging family situations; uncertainties of funding and central office support are annual realities; and the faculty ranges from beginners to veteran teachers. Conversely, the center is atypical in at least the following ways: it is a new building specially designed to support best practices in early childhood education; it is a year-round school; it employs a Family and Community Liaison Coordinator and family support staff; it has an on-site family health clinic; and originally all its teachers were hand-picked for the program through a research-based process. Hinton has clearly contributed to creating a caring environment at the Valeska Hinton Center. As described by teachers Valerie Timmes and Judy Cagle, his leadership also transformed an existing school environment in an old facility into a more caring place. These accomplishments have included problems, setbacks, and tough decisions that some might call uncaring, but a paradoxical reality is that leadership grounded in caring requires toughness.

QUESTIONS FOR PERSONAL REFLECTION

How flexible am I able to be in response to human needs?
How do my typical decision-making processes involve others?
Are caring and fairness compatible values?
What are the principles that ground my decisions?

◄§ 6 §►

Describing a Caring School Leader

The one-caring does not enjoy a caring relationship unless such attention is received and in some way reciprocated by the cared-for. The cared-for does not participate in a caring relationship unless the one-caring chooses to be engrossed in his welfare. The active commitment of each is essential. Similarly, caring leaders inspire the action and dedication of others who are free to choose whether or not to follow. Leaders exist, then, in relationship with followers.

—Jackie M. Blount, "Caring and the Open Moment in Educational Leadership: A Historical Perspective"

KEN HINTON IS A CHALLENGE to capture in words. His caring is a way of being in relationships, an ethical commitment, an expression of love, and a mission. A man with high expectations of himself and others, he is described as soft-spoken. Hinton is also tough and politically astute, with seemingly endless energy, willing to do whatever it takes to make life better for his children and to make the school successful.

LEADING BY EXAMPLE

What does Hinton contribute to making the school environment caring? Quotations from many interviews provide an answer: "By the way he is and does things," said a teacher; "Ken believes in what he is doing, loves what he is doing, and it shows in everything he does," shared a secretary; "He puts himself on the line, being a model he practices what he's teaching. What he asks us to do, he will do. What he asks us not to do, he won't do," emphasized an associate teacher; "Ken is a caring person and cares for the staff and that probably passes down," said another associate teacher. A final quotation provides a summary:

> His caring is as an integral part of the team. He may be the leader but he is not at the top of the mountain. He's right there in the circle

with the rest of us. He cares about children whether they go here or not. He is so caring about the kids and staff, and committed to making life better for all kids in Peoria, not just the children here.

Those interviewed repeatedly used the words *by example* and *as a role model* to describe how Hinton contributes to the caring environment. In other words, they pass on the support and encouragement he offers them. More specifically, a teacher said, "He does the teaming at the building level and then we do the same thing in our villages." Commenting directly on his own belief in the importance of modeling, Hinton said,

> I guess what I am saying is that we give importance to the quality of the relationships that exist not only between teachers, but between teachers and custodians, cafeteria people and custodians, and vice versa, because they are so impacting on what eventually happens to the children, because we model for the children, and if we as adults cannot model what we want them to do it serves no purpose. Basically what I would like to see take place is we need to live what we teach. We need to live what we want the children to do.

I asked Hinton directly how he tries to convey to teachers the importance of caring. He again described modeling, saying that he works "to establish caring as standard behavior through my own interchanges with people, to establish that it is normal to be caring about persons and their needs." He gave as an example a teacher's request to leave the building early to take care of a family-related matter. How would he typically handle that? His preference is that teachers not feel the need to ask permission, but keep him informed and do what they need to do to take care of their own families, even if that may mean leaving school early. "If," he said, "I do not support them in their caring for members of their own family, our efforts as a staff to educate parents about caring for their children become hollow." He is clearly a leader who sees that schools educate more powerfully if words and actions are congruent. Interestingly, Hinton is also seen as modeling imperfections in a way that gives others permission to need help. As one person said,

> Ken is no God. I am not trying to make like he is. When he makes a mistake he will tell us. He is just like anyone else, asks us for advice about how to solve a problem. You don't lean on him as if he's perfect, because he's not. He doesn't want anyone to fail, and we need to encourage him too, because he's a model of this also, of needing to be encouraged.

Although she defines caring as existing within relationships, Noddings (1984) suggests that caring behaviors can be observed. She writes, "When we consider the possibility of institutional caring and what might be meant by the 'caring school,' we shall need to know what to look for" (p. 12). Throughout the analysis, she points out the interaction between the one-caring and the cared-for. Although Hinton himself is quick to acknowledge that persons express caring differently, his behaviors and ways of working and relating with others to establish relationships provide one example of what school leadership grounded in caring looks like. Exhaustive content analysis of the comments and anecdotes offered in the interviews as illustrations of how Hinton contributes to the caring school environment revealed six themes that I express in the following deceptively simple descriptive statements: (1) His use of time reveals his priorities; (2) he supports and encourages others as persons; (3) he listens and solves problems; (4) he keeps the mission focused and central; (5) he does not limit himself or anyone else by or to a role; and (6) he treats every person equally and with respect. Although other interpretations are possible, Hinton's leadership seems best described in terms of Noddings's (1984) essential components of caring: engrossment, action, and reciprocity. I present the six themes of Hinton's leadership in these categories, providing both an interpretation of Noddings's ideas about caring and an illustration of those ideas within the realm of administrative practice.

ENGROSSMENT

One cold, windy Friday, a teacher on her way to another school brought into the office a little boy who had been wandering along MacArthur Highway, the major road running along one side of the school's grounds. She had seen the obviously cold child standing near the busy intersection and guessed that he had wandered away from the Valeska Hinton Center. When she brought him into the office he was wet, filthy, without socks, and dragging a coat caked with mud. He only knew his name and how old he was, but could not tell where he lived. Hinton stopped what he was doing to talk with and comfort the child. He took the boy into the bathroom, cleaned him up, and found dry clothes, including socks and a clean coat. Then Hinton personally took charge of finding out where the child belonged, eventually identifying him through phone calls as a student in a nearby Head Start program. When he delivered the child to the Head Start program, Hinton learned through conversation with the administrators that the child had apparently been left early that morning with a relative who had fallen asleep. The boy, wanting to be at school, had let himself out of the housing project apartment and started walking in the direction of his school, arriving near the Valeska Hinton Center after a walk of many blocks. In spite of his experience of being lost, the child did not ever cry, sensing that he was in a safe place when he was at the center. Although Hinton could have turned caring for this child over to any number of other staff members, he didn't. This introductory example illustrates Hinton's willingness to be engrossed, to put himself and his activities aside to attend to the needs of another, even a child from another school.

Noddings (1984) describes relation as "ontologically basic and the caring relation as ethically basic" (p. 3). Elaborating, she writes that this "means that we recognize human encounter and affective response as a basic fact of human existence" (p. 4). From a focus on that moment of encounter comes her definition of engrossment. Engrossment of the one-caring in the cared-for involves "displacement of interest from my own reality to the reality of the other" (p. 14), or putting oneself aside to focus entirely on another. In other words, Noddings defines engrossment as being fully present in an encounter with another, being receptive of as well as responsive to the cared-for (p. 19). She writes that "at bottom, all caring involves engrossment" (p. 17), implying that engrossment is at the heart of the caring attitude. Again, in Noddings's words, "to the cared-for no act in his behalf is quite as important or influential as the attitude of the one-caring" (pp. 19–20). In the encounter previously described, a busy principal willingly became engrossed in caring for a small lost boy. The following two themes that emerged from the interviews with staff and parents suggest how an attitude of engrossment is characteristic of Hinton's caring: "His use of time reveals his priorities," and "He supports and encourages others as persons."

His Use of Time Reveals His Priorities

If a child, parent, or teacher has a need, Hinton's practice is to drop everything and attend to that person, just as he did for the lost child. Secretary Jackie Petty said,

> I have never heard him say "no" to a person who says, "Could I have a minute?" He always has time, no matter what he is doing, an appointment with the superintendent or any other important meeting. If the building were on fire and a kid said, "Mr. Hinton, I need to ask you a question," he'd sit down and talk.

His actions consistently demonstrate the importance of the children. "The world stops when a child walks into Mr. Hinton's office. He has so many administrative things to worry about, but the children come first," said a teacher. Another teacher described how Hinton once stopped working on a grant that was due that evening to take the time to write a recommendation for a parent who was applying for a job. When the children come into his office before and after school "for hugs and their chats, no matter what is happening he will stop. He will stop and talk with the parents, too," said the home school facilitator. "He is always there for us. I know that I can go to him at any time, or call him at home," said a teacher whose comment is representative of at least a dozen others. Another said, "When I get stressed, I have no problem knocking on his door. Even with piles of paper on the desk he never puts me off, but is always there to listen and give you feedback." The numerous comments about his willingness to stop everything when people need to talk with him show his high regard for people and their needs.

The countless hours Hinton spends at the center demonstrate the devotion that is another aspect of engrossment. Many persons interviewed noted his coming early and staying late, going to all the village functions, and spending time on weekends. One teacher said, "Ken shows that he cares by his commitment to the children, by giving up his time. He doesn't ask us to stay and then he goes home." An associate teacher summed it up with these words:

> He goes above and beyond the call of duty. He inspires us to be a dedicated team because he is so dedicated to what he does. He is like a model for us. He puts in long hours and does anything to keep us happy so we can do our job.

Several others commented on how even his off-duty time "is spent in caring in the community, at different events separate from our school, the Boys' Club and other types of events in the community."

He Supports and Encourages Others as Persons

Hinton's support of others conveys his willingness to encounter them as persons, to become engrossed. Numerous staff members shared examples of Hinton's personal support for anyone confronting a crisis. One teacher received news by phone early one morning that her mother had been hurt in a serious car accident. The children were just arriving in her room when she went to the office upset and wanting to get to the hospital. Hinton drove her to the hospital himself and stayed until he made sure that she and her mother were okay. Another teacher described how Hinton once spent a whole afternoon in a hospital with a child and parent after the child had experienced a seizure. Several persons mentioned his understanding when there had been family illness, including the person who said, "He was thoughtful to me personally when my grandchild died, very supportive." Said a custodian, "He helped me personally through some serious times in my own life." "He cares about everyone here and everybody knows it," said an associate teacher. His consistent friendliness, the "How are you, how is your day going" greeting, also conveys meaningful personal support. "There are a lot of busy people who overlook that sort of thing," volunteered a teacher.

Several teachers spoke of the trust developed through his personal support. One teacher shared,

> He takes an interest in my personal life, too. I could discuss anything with him. I have had some problems and the door was always open for me. He gave me advice and guidance. He will go out on a limb for you. When I was pink-slipped my first two years I knew he would do everything possible to see that I'd be back. When he gives you his word, it's gospel.

Another expressed this same strong level of trust when she said,

> You can talk with him privately and he'll keep it confidential. In other jobs I might have been afraid to talk with someone without feeling stupid or naive about what I am saying—a "should have known" feeling—but I go talk with him and I know I will understand something better and not feel judged.

Hinton also expresses concern for the physical and emotional health of staff members and "cares whether we see our families," said one person. "He values people's emotional commitments" said the lead teacher. He responds to people who are ill or need time off very positively, always saying, "I am supportive of whatever you need to do," said an associate teacher. Another said, "If one of us on the staff gets sick he asks us to go home and take care of ourselves. He cares about the health and safety of the teachers as much as the students." A final example of emotional support is how Hinton handled pink slips, a district termination practice set in motion by yearly funding uncertainties. He called associate teachers to a meeting around lunchtime to hand out the pink slips, even though he could have just put these notifications in their boxes. Reflecting on how his caring, unbureaucratic approach was valued, one of the group said,

I was touched by his taking the time to explain what it meant. He said we were too valuable just to pass out envelopes. I found out later that he gave up going to the Joyce Brothers' community-wide luncheon where he was supposed to get some kind of an award so he could meet with us. He made sure we understood how important we were and that he would be working to get us back.

Almost every staff member interviewed spoke of feeling encouraged and supported by Hinton both personally and professionally. "When I walk into the building I feel respected as a professional but also as a person with a private life that is not always perfect," said a teacher. Another said that Hinton "sees us as individuals with individual needs and takes that into consideration all the time." In slightly different words, "He sees us as individuals, not just a group of teachers." "He's been like a mentor to me. He gave me all the confidence I needed," said one of the first-year teachers. Commenting on the importance of these personal relationships, Hinton said:

In many institutions you might teach for ten or fifteen years next to another teacher and your relationship would be purely professional, and you not know about the person who is next to you. He or she might be going through some traumatic events that might be reshaping his or her life, which might to a certain extent diminish their ability to teach or carry out their responsibilities. However, if I come to work in a supportive environment where I know I am cared for and valued, then I might say something to someone. Someone might extend a hand to me in my time of trial. It makes school more of a humane setting.

ACTION

I watched Hinton go into action when action was called for one morning. He demonstrated that he is a principal who is not content to care *about* persons and their challenges, but is willing to care *for* them. This incident began about 7:15 A.M. one cool fall morning. I had arrived early, but Hinton had been there since 6:30 A.M. We were sitting in his office discussing how he was addressing morale. Perceiving a lowered staff morale, he was in the process of visiting with staff individually and in groups about "where we are in terms of where we want to be." He invited me to sit in on his afternoon visit with the cafeteria staff. Suddenly secretary Jackie Petty rushed through the office's open door to say that a parent was on the phone saying she was "going to give her child away today so don't expect him at school."

Hinton picked up his phone immediately and calmly took charge, hurriedly scrawling Jackie a note asking for the parent's first name. His side of the conversation sounded something like this, with the mother's name interspersed throughout, his voice calmly reassuring:

> Why don't you send him to school today? . . . We can find a place for him to stay for a few days. . . . Would you like that? . . . We can do that. Then you can get a few days' break. . . . Yes, I know he just tries your patience. . . . Why don't you just send him outside and I'll come over and pick him up. Then would you like someone to come talk with you this afternoon? . . . Okay. You send him outside and I'll be there to get him.

Hanging up the phone, Hinton threw on a jacket and asked Jackie to call the Crisis Nursery to see if the facility would have a place for the boy temporarily. He was back at school in 20 minutes with the child, who then happily went off to his class. Although a myriad of other activities filled his morning, Hinton continued to take responsibility for addressing this crisis by making several phone calls. By noon he had arranged for the child to go home with his teacher for the evening. At some point he shared with me that this emotionally unstable mother does this periodically, says she is going to give her child away. Recognizing also that the boy is a challenging child, Hinton is committed to trying to get her help but monitoring the situation carefully. "I don't like to intervene, but if the child's behavior continues to be adversely affected by the mother's behavior, we will intervene," he said.

A social worker whom Hinton had contacted earlier in the day stopped by the school around 2:15 P.M. She had not found the mother. Hinton asked her to persist until she made contact, then to do an assessment to find out if the mother could be dangerous. "We have been following this situation for several years," he told me. He asked the social worker to find out if the previously initiated counseling was still happening, saying he would continue to check with the Crisis Nursery to see if the boy could stay there if a temporary placement became necessary. By 4 P.M. the boy was in the office with his teacher, excited and happy about going to stay overnight at her house. Although Hinton's day contained many other actions, he demonstrated caring in this crisis situation through what he did himself immediately, and seemingly instinctively, as well as through his mobilization of others to protect and care for the child and the mother.

In Noddings's (1984) words, "In the ordinary course of events, we expect some action from one who claims to care, even though action is not all we expect" (p. 10). In addition, she writes that "the acts performed out of caring vary with both situational conditions and type of relationship" (p. 16). Elaborating further, "Our motivation in caring is directed toward the welfare, protection, or enhancement of the cared-for" (p. 243). Hinton's actions in the crisis described certainly fit those criteria. In discussing action, Noddings emphasizes that

> [t]o care is to act not by fixed rule but by affection and regard. It seems likely then that the actions of one-caring will be varied rather than rule-bound. . . . To act as one-caring, then, is to act with special regard for the particular person in a concrete situation. (p. 24)

She discusses how a shift can occur from "I must do something" to "Something must be done," a shift of focus that transforms the cared-for to a problem (p. 24). In the situation I observed, Hinton acted to protect the child, but also initiated action to help the mother. He made a decision, based on the relationship of a particular teacher with a particular child, that it would be in the child's best interest to spend the evening at his teacher's home. Although he could have turned the situation over to a staff person, he responded immediately himself from an "I must do something" imperative. Even though the parent had made this type of threat previously, Hinton referred to her as a person needing help, not as a problem. The next two themes of his leadership indicate that Hinton's caring consistently takes the form of *action*: "He listens and solves problems," and "He keeps the mission focused and central."

He Listens and Solves Problems

One of the cafeteria staff made a direct connection between caring actions and problem-solving when she said, "He is a great person and cares a lot about the kids. You see how he cares because he takes care of problems. By the way he says and does things, you can tell he cares." Another person observed that "he sees needs that maybe other people can't and goes about making positive changes in the lives of kids. He doesn't let situations just remain, but goes about trying to better things for children, staff, for anyone." His writing down even minor problems and taking action in response to them was described by many persons interviewed. As a teacher said, "He follows through with everything." Many spoke of his writing things down and knowing that their concerns would be addressed.

Engaging in dialogue is also a recurrent pattern in Hinton's actions. He routinely engages in dialogue with the staff, particularly to solve problems. Several teachers spoke of his way of listening to their new ideas, talking through their ideas with them, and then encouraging them to try things. "He is willing to let us try something even if he does not think it will work. He listens to all the arguments, then lets us try it. He is open to our way of doing things" is a good summary of what was said. His decision-making processes for anything major typically include careful listening, looking at a situation from all sides, getting input from and involving others, and then taking a problem or concern all the way to resolution, as illustrated in Chapter 5. Said a teacher, "After we toss things around, he goes with the majority most of the time. Sometimes he says, This is the way it will be. That's his job." He talks with staff individually and in groups, "needing to get everyone's opinion before he can be effective," a teacher explained. He encourages and makes time for collaboration and village meetings. Said the head custodian, "We all have a say in what goes on here. So many places don't even ask the opinion of people who will do the job."

Besides asking everyone for an opinion, Hinton can also be counted on to take the children's side, several persons mentioned. Staff described how he seems comfortable with and likes to bring problems and conflicts out in the open so they can talk about things constructively. Similarly, a teacher said, "Ken is always bringing to light what the other person may be feeling in a situation." In helping resolve problems, "He always takes a very positive approach. I have never seen him deal with problems in a negative way. I feel comfortable coming to him with a problem," said an associate teacher. Another associate teacher summarized when she said, "I see Mr. Hinton as a guide who helps pull everything together, and not only from the teachers' viewpoints. A guide takes a lot of input from all, puts it all together, and makes a decision that benefits almost everyone involved."

In addition to responding to problems and gathering opinions when making problem-solving decisions, staff report, Hinton goes the extra mile to solve problems. If he does not know how to resolve a situation, he will find a person who does. If resources are not immediately available, he will find them, and if necessary he will even use his own resources. In addition to supporting teachers' ideas, an associate teacher explained, "When you go to him with a new idea he will work with you to get resources. He tries to get materials that aren't here routinely. He encourages us to do anything that will help the children learn in a better way." In the words of the home school facilitator,

> I've gone to him about quite a few children's needs. He always says don't worry about it. We have the resources. I think often they come from his own pocket. He has said to me that the pupils must have

what they need. He helps work out situations with families and really cares about what happens.

Hinton gives the staff permission to be flexible and make allowances when people have needs. He is a leader who tackles any problem and will always find a way.

He Keeps the Mission Focused and Central

An action more abstract and less concretely visible than problem-solving is keeping the mission of the center focused and central to everyone's actions. One teacher said about Hinton, "He shares vision and brings us together as a team, working together." Another elaborated, "He talks caring to teachers. He brings it out as a value and responsibility to the children." The speech pathologist believes that "Mr. Hinton's philosophy and enthusiasm pervade the entire center." An associate teacher explained,

> He lets us know what he expects for the children, not for himself. None of it is for him but for the children and their families. He's got a beautiful vision. You just want to be part of it. He bases everything on the truth. Even if it might hurt him, he will not lie. The truth keeps the vision going.

"Mr. Hinton's rule is that the children are always first," said the cafeteria manager. A teacher's words provide the best summary:

> His main concern is families and children, that they be content and have what they need. He does not waiver in his commitment to the vision. If I've heard it once I've heard it 1,000 times. We will do what's best for the children. There is a lot of safety and security in working for someone like that.

The vision is not just his, but was a vision several years in the making, its broad outlines developed by the representative community Task Force. Nevertheless, Hinton's total commitment has focused the vision and given it heart. One teacher explained that "the vision is so deeply embedded in all of us. It's what we want for children and families, so that even if we are sometimes overwhelmed, the discussion keeps going." A person from the cafeteria was also articulate: "Everyone's goal is the same. Our vision for the kids is basically the same—healthy, happy children in a safe environment, and excellence. We are all involved in accomplishing these goals." A teacher stated with conviction, "We all hope that this will change our world and the future for our children. That's why we are all here." Such unity of purpose is one reason for the school's unique environment. In the words of a teacher, "In my fifteen years of experience I have never seen such a unified staff, dedicated to the common good. Ken sets the tone and we know he will take the children's side." Staff dedication shows in the warmth and caring they give to the children. "*Our children* is what is emphasized. It is our responsibility to always make parents feel part of the school. He brings that all together," said a teacher.

Hinton's high standards play a role in keeping the mission focused and central. He is a leader who expects a great deal, but gives what he expects. He has high standards for the children, parents, and staff. He has involved the community and serves as a spokesperson for the school in countless ways and arenas. "He is very vocal about child advocacy and encourages this in us by modeling it," said a teacher. "He's a loving person. He's caring and he is totally engrossed in the well-being of the children. You treat the children wrong in any way and you bring down his wrath," said a staff member. Hinton's willingness to be engrossed leads him and others to action.

RECIPROCITY

That Hinton's leadership facilitates and does not block the experience of reciprocity is illustrated in many stories. Hinton told me the following story about how he and the school staff had cared for a parent in need. The story illustrates engrossment, actions of care, and reciprocity.

I don't know how other administrators might respond . . . but it seems like at least once a week a person, teacher or parent, comes to you with a concern or an issue that requires everything else to be pushed aside, because after time and experience you can see that the person is at a point in life where they need your total concentration. For example, we had a parent come to us from another state when we first opened the center. She had two children. One was three and the other a newborn baby. She was here at 6:30 or 7 A.M. in the morning when I walked in, and she would be here late when I was leaving at 6:30 or 7 P.M. just about every evening. This was happening in July.

By early January she was still doing this. She had been working with a variety of people in the building and we have very competent people here who take care of things and make my job very easy. But when her situation got to me she was almost in crisis stage. I remember it was about 1:30 in the afternoon, and the day had been a normal day. She sat in a chair in my office and broke down and cried. She said, "I have no place to go. I have no money," and what she was also saying is, "I don't think anybody cares." I listened and she explained how she had tried this, and tried that, and it hit me at that time why she was always here: she had no home, no place to be.

Asking questions, I learned that she had been living in the public shelters, but she had been to two or three of them already and used up her time, so there was no place else except the streets. So I got on the telephone and started calling around. I called the city, everybody. We were able to find her an emergency place to stay. We pushed everything aside and worked from about 1:30 P.M. until 5:30 or 6 P.M. that evening and we had everything in place. She had a place to go and something to eat, and a place for her and her children to lay their heads that evening. I had the luxury of calling the directors because I know them and through the bureaucracy she got a real nice apartment. There was no furniture, but internally here in the building we got things for her to start her household. We just took that on because we had the ability and the time to do it.

What has happened from this relationship is that she is work-ing, her last child is a student here, and she volunteers in any way she can to give back, to support other parents and children. Every teacher she works with has the benefit of having a supportive parent because our institution is supportive of her, and she in turn has reciprocated.

This parent, cared for, confirmed as a valued person, has grown and re-sponded over time, becoming one-caring herself. Noddings (1984) writes:

> As we examine what it means to care and be cared for, we shall see that both parties contribute to the relation; my caring must be somehow completed in the other if the relation is to be described as caring. This suggests that the ethic to be developed is one of reciprocity. (p. 4)

Noddings (1984) concurs with Buber that reciprocity is not "an iden-tity of gifts given and received," but "what the cared-for gives to the rela-tion either in direct response to the one-caring or in personal delight or in happy growth before her eyes is genuine reciprocity" (p. 74). In the situa-tion described, a dependent and needy young mother has become a self-sufficient and productive citizen who is giving back to the people and the institution that gave to her. Noddings writes of the problem associated with experiencing reciprocity in unequal relationships, stating that particularly when the attitude of warm acceptance and trust is missing, "the one who is the object of caretaking feels like an object. He is being treated, handled by formula" (p. 65). Clearly this was not the case for the homeless young mother, who has been drawn into the circle to become part of the center's family.

A concept closely related to reciprocity is confirmation. Echoing Buber again, Noddings (1984) writes, "I must see the cared-for as he is and as he might be—as he envisions his best self—in order to confirm him" (p. 67). She explains that "When we attribute the best possible motive consonant with reality to the cared-for, we confirm him; that is, we reveal to him an attainable image of himself that is lovelier than that manifested in his present acts" (p. 193), and the confirmation that we offer encourages the person in the direction of that attainable image. Hinton's work with parents is frequently about confirmation. One staff member marveled at his patience with parents whom other principals might dismiss as not worth their time.

When interviewed in 1995, Helm described how fascinating it was to watch Hinton talk with parents about what it means to be a parent. "When he draws a line for them about why they should be doing something as a parent, he always assumes that the parents love the child," she said. As an example, she referred me to the language of a parent newsletter urging parents to take care of getting their children's required immunizations. In the newsletter Hinton wrote, "Please again display your love for your child and take care of this right away." This is an example of attributing the best possible motive to parents in a way that strengthens or confirms them. "His use of language is a powerful attribute that parents respect and respond to," said Helm. Hinton's secretary spoke of the power of his confirmation of others when she said, "He is so positive that you have to be, too. He has a positive spiritual demeanor and sees goodness in everything and everyone. He always looks at the positive. That is contagious if you are around it every day. It rubs off." Describing the effect of Hinton on children, one teacher explained that "The students just adore him. They glow when he comes into the room." Hearing this, I remembered Noddings's (1984) words again: "When the attitude of the one-caring bespeaks caring, the cared-for glows, grows stronger, and feels not so much that he has been given something as that something has been added to him" (p. 20).

Hinton understands that it is not enough to say "I care," that actions must offer caring in a way that honors the mutuality of the relationship. The final two themes reveal that at the heart of Hinton as a leader is not the power of his position, but a genuine attitude of mutuality: "He does not limit himself or anyone else by or to a role," and "He treats every person equally and with respect."

He Does Not Limit Himself or Anyone Else by or to a Role

Noddings (1984) has written, "Whatever I do in life, whomever I meet, I am first and always one-caring or one cared-for. I do not 'assume roles' unless I become an actor" (p. 175). Hinton does not approach being a principal as an opportunity to be in a traditional principal's role. He does not "act" as principal. For example, he does not use the power of his position to make arbitrary decisions. Family and Community Liaison Coordinator Burke emphasized this point in describing her working relationship with Hinton. "Ken will ask me before he does things. He cares about my opinion. He would always get my input, for example, before enrolling a child. He would never just make the decision himself." Professional Development Coordinator Helm talked about how she, Burke, and Hinton function as an administrative team. "What is here is so complex. There are many things Ken does that no principal would do. Roles here are overlapping. It is not a traditional principal's role."

Other faculty and staff provided many illustrations of how Hinton steps outside of the traditional principal's role. They mentioned his helping with cleanup after special programs, buying children shoes with his own money, using the school washer and dryer himself to take care of cleaning clothes for children, braiding a girl's hair, pulling weeds with the custodians when it was 102 degrees, changing and cleaning up children who have accidents, hauling the soda pop and filling the machines, subbing for teachers, fixing the copy machine, and helping out in the kitchen, to list just a few examples. Although several persons saw him as a father figure in the school, others called him leader, fellow teacher, colleague, and friend. One associate teacher described how children respond to Hinton: "He's like a magnet. The children want to connect with him. They can touch him and talk with him. He's not just a figurehead, 'the principal.'" A teacher said something similar: "I see him as human, not just a principal." Another teacher told about her first week at the school: "I had a bad day and I was completely distraught, but I didn't feel foolish to be in his office in tears. It was like talking to a more experienced friend." Teachers and others appreciate the welcoming office atmosphere. In the words of a teacher, "Ken does not have professional distance."

Hinton's willingness to do whatever needs to be done to make the children and the school successful creates a ripple effect, one teacher explained. "He does not say, That's not my job. He's done everything. When you see someone that high up doing anything and everything, it inspires the rest of the staff to follow suit." Hinton also articulates the importance of everyone doing what needs to be done. One teacher reported that he devoted time at a recent faculty meeting to the idea that "nothing is just someone else's job and not yours." He puts the emphasis on "taking care of all the children, not just those in your classroom," said an associate teacher. She continued:

> We are not just teachers in our classrooms, but in the whole school. If a child from another village is running in the hall, or if a child is wandering, or crying, or upset, we are encouraged to stop and see where the child should be.

It is not only the teachers who have internalized this value, observed a person from the family support office:

> The secretaries are part mothers, grandmothers, aunts—not just secretaries. If a child comes in with a sad face, they push the secretary job aside and give the child love. Even a maintenance man drilling a hole will stop if a child comes in crying and will attend to the child, or attend to a parent needing advice.

When the principal responds as a caring person to a whole variety of human needs and is not confined to acting from or within a role, then everyone else in the building is empowered to care.

He Treats Every Person Equally and with Respect

Hinton regards all people as important and deserving of respect regardless of age, position, or economic status. "He treats each of us as if we were as important as anyone, regardless of what we do or our titles. He treats us with respect and dignity and makes each feel as important as the next," explained a secretary. A total of 30 of the people interviewed made this same point in describing how Hinton contributes to the caring environment. Following are a few examples: "He shows genuine respect to everyone who comes in the building," said one teacher, whereas an associate teacher put it, "I have never seen Ken treat one child different from another, not a child or a parent." Looking from another angle, a teacher said, "He loves kids completely and that love causes kids to give him respect. The staff and kids both respect him more than other principals I've known." A person who works in the cafeteria said, "Kids are from difficult home settings, but he does not treat one person better than the other, he treats them all the same." A parent said, "He accepts and adopts these children as his own."

The respect continues even when Hinton disagrees with a teacher or is disciplining a child. A staff member explained, "If you're wrong he will discuss it with you, speak to you about it, but his delivery is in such a way that you almost thank him for it." Several mentioned how he never raises his voice and still gets his point across. One person commented that "if he does not like something, he will say something once in a positive way and you will never hear about it again." Another teacher said, "Ken constantly lets me be me and my children be children, yet redirects my children and me when I need it in a firm but kind way, never demeaning or belittling." Children coming to the office for disciplinary reasons usually get hugs as well as questions and a talk. One staff member described taking a couple of kids in for discipline:

> He started out with a hug and said how nice it was to see each child. Then he got down on their level and asked questions, what could they have done differently—not preaching, but trying to teach them to be in charge of themselves.

Valeska Hinton Center parents also receive respect from everyone, beginning with Hinton. In the words of the home school facilitator, "He encourages us to have respect for parents and to encourage parents to participate because he feels they are an important part of the school." "I have never seen a child or a parent turned away because they didn't fit in. Everyone is made to feel welcome," explained a member of the family support office staff. Said a teacher, "Parents feel confident that they can come here with a problem and get some help, not as charity but because they are cared about." Respect that facilitates reciprocity is at the heart of Hinton. A custodian's words provide a summary: "It's how he treats people that I really admire."

HINTON'S DEFINITION OF LEADERSHIP

Hinton views the principalship as a nurturing role. In explaining his choice of *nurturing* as the one word that would best describe the environment of the school, Hinton said that "persons who work with children need to know they are loved, respected and cared for before they can really make an impact on the lives of children." He believes that high-quality, meaning-ful, and personal relationships with faculty and staff are more than busi-ness or professional relationships. Such relationships are about "enhancing the being or the purpose or the life of the individual." Hinton believes that nurturing is an integral part of both learning and human development, for adults as well as children.

Whereas many are quick to acknowledge the importance of caring to teaching, and "the most recent research does reveal an intentional caring as pedagogy" (Eaker-Rich & Van Galen, 1996, p. 2), how many see intentional caring as an aspect of leadership? Hinton definitely does. Asked to define leadership, he answered:

> I think leadership is the ability of a person to take on an objective and achieve that objective, and in so doing, in the process of working with others who are working with you on that objective, being approachable, cooperative, and respected. You have to be caring about those with whom you work. It takes a great deal of strength and integrity. I've also found leadership in certain respects to be lonely. You lead by example, and it requires that you have an understanding of the task at hand, and an understanding of the personalities of those you work for and of those you work with.

Courtney and Noblit (1994) assert that "the caring perspective refocuses us on the relationships between people as the key element in education" (p. 67). Hinton, his leadership grounded in uncommon caring, would agree.

QUESTIONS FOR PERSONAL REFLECTION

How do I handle conflicting demands for my time?
To what am I unalterably committed?
Do I respect the inherent worth and dignity of all persons?
How do I show others that I care?

❧ 7 ☙

Can Caring Leadership Enhance Learning?

We think by feeling. What is there to know?
                    —Theodore Roethke, "The Waking"

IN LINKING THOUGHT and feeling, the American poet Theodore Roethke anticipated the discoveries of cognitive neuroscientists and the call for a renewed emphasis on the role of emotion in learning. For example, Greenspan (1997), a child psychiatrist and medical school professor, argues that we must base our educational methods on a developmental model, identifying the following as its key tenet: "*Intellectual learning shares common origins with emotional learning. Both stem from early affective interactions. Both are influenced by individual differences, and both must proceed in a stepwise fashion, from one developmental level to another*" (p. 219), for children to reach their true intellectual potential. According to Greenspan, if children have been deprived of the opportunity to relate to others with warmth and trust, then the role of the school must be to furnish them with experiences to develop these capacities if we want them to grow emotionally and intellectually. He cautions educators not to separate cognitive and emotional intelligence.

Staff at the Valeska Hinton Center understand that emotional and cognitive learning are linked and that learning experiences must be developmentally appropriate. Staff define learning broadly to include attitudes, skills, and knowledge developed by the total program to accomplish the broad academic, social, and emotional goals of the school. Whether learning is primarily about remembering or understanding has long been debated. "Traditionally, learning has been thought to be a 'mimetic' activity" (Brooks & Brooks, 1993, p. 15) requiring students to repeat back to teachers on tests and quizzes the "new" information that teachers had previously presented to them. By this definition, also called the banking concept of education (Freire, 1992, p. 58), learning means acquiring new information deposited in the brain by the instructor, and the evidence of learning becomes what is remembered. A constructivist approach to learning, on the other hand, puts emphasis on understanding, on students creating their own knowledge. For example, Brooks and Brooks (1993) argue "that we learn by constructing new understandings of relationships and phenomena in our world" (p. 5). Teachers must help students build these new understandings, however, on their prior experiences.

A comprehensive discussion of what is known about how learning occurs in the brain is beyond the scope of this chapter, although consideration of the role of emotion in learning will suggest that caring may influence learning (Caine & Caine, 1991; Damasio, 1994; Sylwester, 1995; LeDoux, 1996; Jensen, 1998). Caring has long been considered critical to teaching. The important question underlying this chapter, however, is whether caring leadership enhances learning. In other words, can a principal's caring be "demonstrated in substantive ways that translate into student learning" (Sergiovanni, 1994, p. 145)? In this chapter I explore answers to this question by considering implications of brain research; evidence that Valeska Hinton Center students experience enhanced academic, social, and emotional learning; and Hinton's beliefs about the link between caring and learning.

IMPLICATIONS OF BRAIN RESEARCH

Cognitive neuroscience is a name given to the work of an interdisciplinary group of researchers studying the brain. Keeping up with the research in this fast-moving field is challenging. Much of the research is either highly specialized or focused on the understanding and treatment of disease, and therefore not of general interest to educators. Indeed, as Jensen (1998) suggests, "Brain research doesn't necessarily 'prove' anything. It merely suggests ideas or paths that have a higher probability of success" (p. 6). Practicing and future school leaders, whether in the classroom or the principal's office, must consider for themselves whether research on learning and the brain supports the argument that caring leadership may enhance learning. Examining just one aspect of this research, what the cognitive neuroscientists themselves have written about the role of emotion in learning, deepens understanding of why educators and others are paying attention.

Cognitive Neuroscientists' Perspectives

Antonio Damasio is a professor and head of the Neurology Department at the University of Iowa College of Medicine. In *Descartes' Error* (1994), he explores evidence that emotion is involved in all our reasoning. "I propose that human reason depends on several brain systems, working in concert across many levels of neuronal organization, rather than a single brain center" (p. xiii), he writes. "Feelings, along with the emotions they come from, are not a luxury. They serve as internal guides" (p. xv) that influence our rational behavior in important ways. He recounts experiences of patients who, as a result of having a prefrontal portion of the brain damaged, experience loss of the capacity to feel but have no apparent impairment of cognitive processes. However, in example after example these patients then have enormous difficulty with decision-making. Formerly functioning normally, they now make decisions seen as socially unacceptable or at least qualitatively different from their former lives. They become incapable of planning and taking care of basic needs. Their acquired deficits of reasoning and decision-making strongly suggest that "certain aspects of the process of emotion and feeling are indispensable for rationality" (p. xiii), according to Damasio. To summarize, because feelings and reason are importantly intertwined, we need emotions to make good decisions. The body and its emotions cannot be split from the workings of the mind. "This is Descartes' error: the abyssal separation between body and mind" (p. 249), he concludes.

Joseph LeDoux is a professor at the Center for Neural Science at New York University. He presents several themes about the nature of emotions in *The Emotional Brain* (1996). Three ideas seem particularly relevant to caring leadership: that certain neural memory pathways created early in life are irreversible, that long-term stress can impair memory, and that emotions overpower reason neurologically. LeDoux arrived at the concept of irreversible memory pathways through extensive study of the fear system of the brain. According to his research, fear is an emotional response that maximizes chances of survival (p. 128), and the fear conditioning all humans experience creates fear triggers (p. 141). LeDoux states that "unconscious fear memories established through the amygdala appear to be indelibly burned into the brain. They are probably with us for life" (p. 252). LeDoux provides evidence that because of these neural memory pathways, "emotional responses are, for the most part, generated unconsciously" (1996, p. 17), and naturally overpower reason:

> While conscious control over emotions is weak, emotions can flood consciousness. This is so because the wiring of the brain at this point in our evolutionary history is such that connections from the emotional systems to the cognitive systems are stronger than connections from the cognitive systems to the emotional systems. (p. 19)

This biological reality provides insights into why students whose emotions are aroused are often not in control of their behaviors. Jensen (1998) builds on LeDoux's insights when he explains why calling a student to the principal's office does not always have the desired effect. "If a student is about to be called to the principal's office, the body's stress and threat response kicks in. Pulse is up, skin is flushed, and the body's on 'edge.' A change in chemicals means a likely change in behaviors" (Jensen, 1998, p. 44). A student's out-of-control defensiveness in this situation may be a survival response triggered by fear and based on years of neural patterning.

LeDoux describes the hippocampus as "a key player in the game of memory" (1996, p. 189). Experiments with laboratory rats have shown that

> [i]f stress persists too long the hippocampus begins to falter in its ability to control the release of the stress hormones, and to perform its routine functions. Stressed rats are unable to learn and remember how to perform behavioral tasks that depend on the hippocampus. (p. 240)

Over a prolonged time "severe but temporary stress can result in a shriveling up of the dendrites in the hippocampus" (p. 242). The human hippocampus is also vulnerable to too much stress. Clearest evidence comes from experiences of Vietnam veterans or victims of repeated childhood abuse. Both may "exhibit significant deficits in memory ability without any loss in IQ or other cognitive functions" (p. 242). LeDoux further clarifies this point: "Memory is likely to be enhanced by mild stress, due to the facilitatory effects of adrenaline, but may be interfered with if the stress is sufficiently intense and prolonged to raise the level of adrenal steroids to the point where the hippocampus is adversely affected" (pp. 243–244). He also asserts that "the prefrontal cortex, like the hippocampus, may be altered by stress" (p. 250). This research on the effects of stress suggests, in Sylwester's words, that "emotionally stressful school environments are counterproductive because they can reduce the students' ability to learn" (1995, p. 77).

LeDoux's work reinforces the value of a caring school environment. He illustrates human susceptibility at an unconscious level to fear triggers and stress responses that can shut down learning. He paints a picture of a brain at the mercy of early emotional patterning and demonstrates how powerfully emotions affect both memory and behaviors. His book strongly suggests that an environment students experience as fearful is not likely to enhance their learning. As if responding to this implication, a Valeska Hinton Center teacher expressed her understanding that a caring environment feels safe. "We show the children lots of love and caring and this gives them an enthusiastic attitude about school. When they see teachers caring so much, that says to them that this is a safe nurturing environment," she said.

Educators' Perspectives

Caine and Caine (1991), Sylwester (1995), and Jensen (1998) have written about implications of brain research for educators. The brain research finding that emotion plays an important role in learning through its links with attention and memory has been given wide exposure by Sylwester and others in educational journals and conference presentations. In one of the first books to present implications of brain research for educators, Caine and Caine (1991) explain that "the brain does not separate emotions from cognition, either anatomically or perceptually" (p. vii). Abbott (1997) similarly states that "effective learning depends on emotional energy" (p. 8). According to Sylwester (1995), recent research on brain processes has verified that "emotion is very important to the educative process because it drives attention, which drives learning and memory" (p. 72). This statement of Sylwester's is frequently quoted, but what does he mean? He does not say that emotion causes learning, nor that only positive emotional responses may activate learning. He does say that "it's biologically impossible to learn anything that you're not paying attention to; the attentional mechanism drives the whole learning and memory process" (1997, p. 17). Emotional responses activate the attention of students who may then respond either negatively or positively, perceiving either a danger or an opportunity.

Caine and Caine (1991) address the role of a supportive environment in learning. A supportive caring environment, they explain, minimizes both the reality and the perception of threat, thereby contributing to the relaxed alertness that facilitates learning. "The brain appears to be very much like a camera lens: the brain's 'lens' opens to receive information when challenged, when interested, or when in an 'innocent,' childlike mode and closes when it perceives threat that triggers a sense of helplessness" (Caine & Caine, 1991, p. 63). Jensen (1998) elaborates on the impact of socially stressful environments, saying that "excess stress and threat in the school environment may be the single greatest contributor to impaired academic learning" (p. 52). Sylwester's assertion that "emotionally stressful school environments are counterproductive because they can reduce the students' ability to learn" (1995, p. 77) also implies an indirect link between the reduced stress of a caring environment and learning.

Seeming to speak directly to what principals can do to enhance learning, Caine and Caine write:

> Because it is impossible to isolate the cognitive from the affective domain, the emotional climate in the school and classroom must be monitored on a consistent basis. . . . In general, the entire environment needs to be support-

ive and marked by mutual respect and acceptance both within and beyond the classroom. (1991, p. 82)

Alluding to the indirect contribution of the principal to a supportive environment, Caine and Caine state:

Some of the most significant experiences in a student's life are fleeting "moments of truth," such as a chance encounter in a corridor with a relatively unknown teacher or, possibly, a "distant" administrator. These brief communications are often instinctive. Their emotional color depends on how "real" and profound the support of teachers, administrators, and students is for one another. (pp. 82–83)

In other words, the emotional climate of a school, if it is colored by care, will provide the support of mutual respect and acceptance that may enhance a student's ability to learn and remember. Furthermore, Jensen (1998) writes, "when we feel valued and cared for, our brain releases the neurotransmitters of pleasure: endorphins and dopamine. This helps us enjoy our work more" (p. 33). Students who enjoy school are more willing to pay attention and more open to learning.

Connections between emotion and learning suggest that a leader grounded in caring walks a path with a higher probability of success and will make a substantive contribution to student learning by building a supportive, caring environment. If caring leadership can contribute to an environment that will make the difference between positive school experiences that may enhance learning and negative school experiences that contribute to stress and alienation, then certainly nurturing a caring environment ought to be a primary focus of school principals. Particularly for many at risk students, a caring environment makes school a sanctuary in which learning can proceed without the constant fear that restricts their lives in so many ways.

VALESKA HINTON CENTER LEARNING OUTCOMES

"This school has a very special environment with high expectations and high goals, excitement, positive feelings. You just know it has to be related to the administrator," one teacher explained to me as she talked about how Hinton influenced the environment. Another teacher expressed enthusiasm for teaching at the center when she said, "The school is unique in that there are very few schools that exist today that provide young children opportunities to develop in areas of social, emotional, and academic skills." The words of a third teacher provide a summary:

We work together to see that this is a good place for children to learn. They feel comfortable and the parents feel comfortable. That parents and families feel comfortable here is a huge part of the success we have achieved so far.

Assessing Academic Learning

The overall goal of the curriculum is to have all children leave the center able to do second grade work in their neighborhood schools. The academic learning goals are significant and require the commitment of everyone in the building. As one teacher said, "If everyone in the building did not care, we couldn't achieve as much as we have, and wouldn't strive to do everything we do." An associate teacher explained the effort this way: "We are always trying different teaching techniques to help the children learn better. The school is open to new ways. Ken encourages us to do anything to help the children learn in a better way." Students' grades and achievement test scores when they leave the center to attend their neighborhood schools are one indicator of whether the overall goal has been met.

Grade Analysis. The first children to graduate from the Valeska Hinton Center began second grade in the fall of 1995. Hinton has continued to follow the progress of the children and been gratified by their grades. At the end of the 1997–98 school year, he compiled grade information for 140 children who had graduated from the center and were in grades two, three, and four in the Peoria public schools. The students in the group were 80.7% low-income, free or reduced-price lunch; were 60.0% African American, 36.4% White, and 3.6% Hispanic; and were 55.7% male and 44.3% female. Second graders were averaging Bs in all subject areas. Third graders were at the B level in spelling, conduct, and effort, and at the C+ level in reading, language arts, and math. Fourth graders were at the B level in every area except math. These grades indicate that the children were succeeding at a high level with the regular curriculum.

Grade data from the former Valeska Hinton Center students were also analyzed for answers to three other questions: Do any mean GPA differences exist between boys and girls? Do any mean GPA differences exist between African Americans and Whites? Do any mean GPA differences exist in the sex-by-race interaction? The questions were answered by using a 2 × 2 between-subjects analysis of variance (ANOVA). GPA was calculated using reading, spelling, language arts, and math grades. There was a statistically significant difference between boys and girls, with girls having a higher mean GPA (3.04) than boys (2.71). However, no statistically significant mean GPA differences existed between African Americans and

Whites, and the sex-by-race interaction did not yield statistically signifi-cant mean GPA differences. The grade data analysis is generally encour-aging, particularly the absence of significant differences between African Americans and Whites, but further study is required before any conclu-sions can be drawn. (Refer to Table A.1 in the Appendix for mean GPAs by academic subject, conduct, and effort for the three grades.)

Achievement Test Analysis. At Hinton's request, Dr. Paul Holmes, Peoria public schools Director of Research, Evaluation, and Testing, has under-taken a longitudinal study of *Iowa Tests of Basic Skills* scores of former Valeska Hinton Center students. The two questions driving the analysis are (1) Do any achievement test score differences exist between Valeska Hinton Center students and students in a control group? and (2) Do achievement test score gains of Valeska Hinton students last over time? Holmes completed both a cohort group analysis and grade-level analy-sis of four sets of achievement test data from four groups of students. These groups in the 1997–98 academic year included the current Valeska Hinton Center first graders and former Valeska Hinton Center students who are now in second, third, and fourth grades in their neighborhood schools. Control group students were randomly selected from students at the same grade levels in another Title I primary school in the district. (Refer to Figure A.1 in the Appendix for the longitudinal study model.)

The Peoria public schools administer *Iowa Tests of Basic Skills* yearly in early October for students in all grades in Title I primary schools, and for students in grades one and three in the district's other primary schools. Holmes restricted the cohort groups to students for whom the district had yearly scores, thus limiting the cohorts to students who were attending Title I schools. Cohort analysis of the achievement test scores revealed no significant differences between Valeska Hinton Center students and the control group students. Statistically significant differences revealed through grade-level analysis, however, suggest that students who completed 3 or 4 years (student entry into the preprimary program may have been at age 3 or 4) at the Valeska Hinton Center before entering their neighborhood schools significantly outperform control group students on the *Iowa Tests of Basic Skills*. (Refer to Figure A.2 in the Appendix for a grade-level com-parison of ITBS Reading Grade Equivalent Mean Scores.) Holmes finds the data encouraging and hopeful. Whereas no definitive statement can yet be made, Holmes hypothesizes that continuation of the longitudinal study for 2 more years may yield statistically significant results that will confirm the program's success through both the cohort analysis and grade-level analysis procedures. The lack of significant differences in the 1994–98 cohort analysis data may be related to differences in the effectiveness of the program when the school first opened compared with its effectiveness beginning with year three (1995–96) of implementation. Continuation of the longitudinal study will also reveal whether the gains emerging through grade-level analysis hold up over time. Besides length of time in the program, two other factors that may affect achievement test results are the center's year-round schedule compared with the traditional calendar followed by other schools, and the higher level of parent involvement at the center than exists in most other Title I schools.

Stanines provide another way of looking at the achievement test results. In 1994, the center's first graders (Cohort Group 1) had an NCE (Normal Curve Equivalent) score of 49.5 on the Iowa Tests of Basic Skills in Reading, equivalent to the 5.0 stanine. In 1995, the center's first graders (Cohort Group 2) had an NCE of 50.5 in Reading, again placing their performance at the 5.0 stanine. Performance at the 5.0 stanine level is considered average. Hinton explained that typical reading scores for a Title I school would be around the fourth or fifth stanines. The 1996 NCE for the center's first graders was 67.2, equivalent to performance at the 7.3 stanine level. Scores at this level are considered to be above average, and perhaps indicate the cumulative effect of the school's curriculum, caring environment, and parent involvement focus. For these children in their third or fourth year at the school to score at the seventh stanine in reading indicates that the program is having measurable results, in Hinton's opinion.

"Test scores don't necessarily reflect the level and degree of caring, but they do to some extent," Hinton believes. Even though preliminary results from the district's longitudinal study are inconclusive, they validate for Hinton the decision in 1995–96 to keep first grade at the center. He expects the longitudinal study to eventually confirm that for students who are in the Valeska Hinton Center program for 4 years, a significant difference in academic achievement will exist throughout their school careers. If designing the school again, Hinton would begin the program with 2-year-olds and extend it through fourth grade to ensure maximum gains for students.

Documenting Social and Emotional Learning

A family support associate expressed the school's social and emotional goals well:

> The philosophy behind the school is teaching children how to be secure within themselves, allowing children to make decisions, take responsibility for their actions, learning they are all individuals, learning ways to deal with anger, about the emotions they might have, how to calm down on their own.

A specific Valeska Hinton Center goal that supports social and emotional development is that "the children will develop comfortable, empathetic interactions with all people." How does empathy develop? Greenspan (1997) offers this opinion:

> The feeling of being cared for and caring for others eventually becomes the basis for empathy. . . . We learn about empathy and compassion not from what we're told but from how we're treated. We can be told a hundred times a day to be kind and compassionate. Parents may see themselves as role models and point out their compassion toward others, but their words will be empty unless their children have experienced their caring and concern. (pp. 119–120)

An associate teacher agrees and explains how teachers play a role. She said,

> By caring ourselves, we try to teach them to care for each other. We focus on this in our classrooms so that they will take caring outside classroom to family members and others. If we teach that one thing, it will be worth it.

Testimonials of teachers and parents provide the best evidence that social and emotional learning occurs. Several spoke about how the children are learning to manage their emotions. "When my son and another boy were having problems, Ken brought the two boys into the conference room and invited me to observe," said the cafeteria manager. "He talked with them but never raised his voice, just altered his tone to stress certain things. They ended up being friends, shook hands, gave each other a hug and hugged him. He told them they were both his kids." A secretary was enthusiastic about what she had seen children learn. "In the year I have been here the numbers of children I've seen progress, move, change—it's just been wonderful. For example, one small boy would run out of the building if he got angry, but not anymore." A family support associate described the outcomes of a particular curricular program used at the center:

> With the Second Step violence prevention program, teachers talk to kids about things. The talking helps the children see they can use words. They don't have to hit. They learn to reason themselves, see what could they have done differently. "See that face of the person you hurt?" a teacher will ask. "What could you do differently? What will you do now?" Kids respond to the family atmosphere of love and patience. I'd love to see these kids later when they take this training into society.

Several commented on social learning outcomes. "If teachers didn't care, or staff, or Mr. Hinton, the center wouldn't be as successful. In the morning you see how much everyone cares. The children are happy to be here. You very seldom see an unhappy child," said one of the parents who works in the cafeteria. She added, "I feel fortunate to have my children here," continuing with these words of praise for the program:

> Without this place my children would be doing fine academically, but because of the center they are socially mature for their ages. Cooperation is important. In other schools they do not take or have time to teach something like anger management. This is something that will stay with them forever and they will be able to build on those skills. When a child is new here you can see the difference. They are not as socially open. Parents learn about anger management, too, along with their children.

In another example of social learning, a staff member explained that she saw the children become like family:

> Children take sibling roles with each other. You see fighting and you also see children sticking up for each other, saying, "You can't do that," teaching and protecting each other. Especially the older children are this way with the younger. When they have the same friends for four years in their villages a special bond develops.

Besides emotional and social skills, the center develops children's self-esteem. An associate teacher gave the best description of how that happens:

> The kids need and get stability here. I see such a change in the kids. We see them come in with heads down, no self-esteem, and they walk out with heads high, proud of themselves and what they have done. They have self-confidence to whip the world. I have four-year-olds just bouncing to read. The children are lacking a lot in their lives, but here they are safe, and they really respond to this environment.

A teacher commented on the underlying acceptance that facilitates the growth of self-esteem when she said, "We are consumed with children's strengths, not with what they can't do. We work together, like a family. We have a lot of children here with terrible home lives, but while they are here, they are different and special." The building; the program, with its village structure; and the academic, social, and emotional goals are all designed to promote learning. Elaborating on the powerful role of emotions in learning, Jensen (1998) writes:

> Some still believe that learning and emotions are at opposite ends of the spectrum. It's time for all of us to catch up on the research. . . . The affective side of learning is the critical interplay between how we feel, act, and think. There is no separation of mind and emotions; emotions, thinking, and learning are all linked. (p. 71)

HINTON'S BELIEFS ABOUT CARING AND LEARNING

Hinton's beliefs about how his caring affects teaching and learning are based on his observations, experiences, and reading of research. We talked on more than one occasion about his perceptions of how he contributes to learning.

Caring Leadership Supports Caring by Teachers

Hinton believes that his personal relationships with teachers contribute to their ability to care for the students and their families. Caring relationships may not be an ingredient in traditional definitions of instructional leadership, but Hinton consciously offers love, respect, and care to the faculty. Hinton's leadership, particularly his keeping the mission focused and central, reinforces teachers' understanding that what they do is important. "In so many other institutions there is a separation, an impersonality, the attitude that 'this is a job' and 'I have learning outcomes that have to be met,'" Hinton said. At the Valeska Hinton Center, teaching is definitely more than a job.

Hinton believes that as an adult, a person "can't be a full individual without having a purpose and a reason for being." He elaborated, "I think teachers have to like what they are doing, have to feel good about themselves, and feel there is a purpose and there is a meaning to what they do." They also have to feel valued as individuals. Hinton takes the time to reinforce in countless ways that he values and cares for teachers, building relationships over time by supporting and encouraging them as persons and professionals. He says,

> My own experience as a teacher taught me that there is an aspect of a human being that has to be filled before a person can move on to the next step. . . . Human beings need to know they are loved, respected, and cared for before you can really make an impact on their lives.

"In other words, you are saying that helping teachers become more clear about the meaning of their lives and their work, that building relationships, *precedes* what gets accomplished with the curriculum?" I asked. Hinton's answer was a clear yes:

> It is important that I value a person for what he or she does, for what he or she believes, that the person is given room to make errors and realize that he or she is accepted as an individual. . . . Once you have established those relationships and teachers, parents and the other people with whom you work know that you care and that you're involved, and let's don't skirt the word, that there is love—then they know that they will be protected, and they become free to grow.

Hinton believes that learning and individual growth result when teachers are valued. The teachers become free to take risks and to explore how to reach individual students. They adopt teaching practices that are more caring, more individualized, and more equitable, he explained.

Hinton believes that the climate, or environment, of the Valeska Hinton Center is a direct result of caring relationships among everyone at the school, whatever their roles. "It is like a family relationship, that we have a responsibility to and for each other," he said. "That sense of teaming, family, collaboration, coalition, or whatever word you want to use, is critical in seeing that children succeed, because so many kids are not given examples of genuine concern and caring by adults." The children are learning about caring from the adults in the school. "Relationships are important because we are modeling for the children and what we do impacts what eventually happens to them," he explained. Through caring relationships that empower teachers to grow personally and professionally, to become better teachers, Hinton contributes indirectly to student learning.

Caring Teachers Are More Successful

In his 30 years as an educator, Hinton has known many teachers. He has hired teachers, encouraged teachers, watched teachers succeed and fail, been inspired himself by teachers, and let some teachers go. Hinton believes that caring of teachers for students and their families definitely enhances learning, particularly for low-income and minority students. Teachers who are successful with students in this environment are the ones whose caring shows in their work. Hinton believes that teachers who either allow themselves to care or learn to care change their instructional practices. "Caring carries with it a loss of class, ethnicity, gender, and religion," he said. "If a teacher cares, then these things that separate us through igno-rance and fear become unimportant. Status ceases to matter, and children are simply children." Comfort with diversity allows teachers to extend caring to the families of their students, to build partnerships with parents that enhance students' learning.

With care, Hinton has observed, teachers move from a broad focus on lesson plans and their class as a whole to more of an individual focus on each student's personal growth. Teachers become more willing to pay at-tention to charting and documenting a student's personal development. They are more willing to individualize, to develop projects and learning experiences that respond to children's needs and interests, to do portfolio assessment. Children learn more in an environment where teachers see each child as an individual person with his or her own learning styles and needs, Hinton believes. "Learning is intellectual and mental, but it is also emo-tional and physical in terms of the way persons learn. If a door is shut in terms of a teacher and caring, then that teacher's work with that student is almost counterproductive." Ultimately, caring affects the quality of a student's learning, Hinton asserts:

> You can teach someone if you don't care, but the depth, longevity, and meaning of it are greatly affected. . . . When I have teachers who care for the children they teach, I can see a night-and-day difference in academic performance, in discipline, in how the teacher is perceived by the parents of the child. I have validated it, looked at test scores and seen that students perform better. The child's perception of learning, of themselves, and the world is altered. Failure is not an option.

Hinton's belief that caring teachers are more successful has many sources. Being a principal has helped crystallize this belief, but clearly the roots are in his experiences as a teacher and learner himself. Both of these perspectives validate for him the link between caring and learning. As a child, Hinton experienced how the level of caring by teachers played a role in his openness to learning at school. In his first teaching position, before any learning could happen, Hinton had to get the attention of a class gone wild. First he cared enough to fight for their attention; then, by involving their parents and demonstrating caring about whether they learned or not, he succeeded in creating a classroom learning community. Another teacher in the same building where he began his career greatly influenced Hinton's belief in the power of caring teaching. "Miss Laurice Joseph is a woman who taught seventh and eighth grades for forty-plus years, most of them in a tough junior high environment," he said. "I still worship the ground

she walks on. In all that time," he explained, "she never missed a basketball game. She was always there. She was about five feet, four inches tall,
but I've seen her take the biggest kids in the school and say, 'Now bend
down here. I need to fuss at you.'" They accepted the fussing because they
knew she cared:

> Whenever a child had a birthday, in their desk would be a card and
> a little letter. If a child did something wrong on a paper, there
> would not be a big fat red F on the paper, but a note saying, "See
> me. We need to talk about your grammar." She was able to accom-
> plish things with students that dumbfounded the other teachers. It
> was because the children knew from the first day that "If I'm upset
> with you it's because I want you to be somebody." That was articu-
> lated by the way she did things, what she said, even the way she
> walked.

Laurice Joseph gave Hinton many lessons in the power of caring to bring
about learning even with the most difficult of students. As a principal, he
continues to incorporate these lessons into his own work as an educator.
When he is hiring a teacher, he looks for "Laurice Joseph qualities" of overt,
loving, and persistent caring.

LEARNING GROUNDED IN CARING

"The heart of caring in schools is relationships with others," Sergiovanni
writes (1994, p. 145). Several approaches to whether caring leadership
can enhance learning have been offered in this chapter. That learning is
grounded in emotions seems to have been clearly established in the 1990s,
suggesting a link between caring school environments and learning
(Caine & Caine, 1991; Damasio, 1994; Sylwester, 1995; LeDoux, 1996;
Greenspan, 1997; Elias et al., 1997; Jensen, 1998). Quantitative analysis of
grades and achievement test scores as well as qualitative evidence document academic, social, and emotional learning. Former Valeska Hinton
Center students are experiencing success in their neighborhood schools,
although causal links between that success and the center's caring environment cannot yet be established. Hinton believes that caring teachers are
more successful and that through his caring relationships he influences the
learning of staff, students, and parents.

Elias et al. (1997) state: "[W]hen schools attend systematically to students' social and emotional skills, the academic achievement of children
increases, the incidence of problem behaviors decreases, and the quality

of the relationships surrounding each child improves" (p. 1). Their language in this passage echoes Hinton's beliefs about why caring is important to learning:

> We work better when we care and when we are cared about, and so do students. Caring is a spoken or an unspoken part of every interaction that takes place in classrooms, lunchrooms, hallways, and playgrounds. Children are emotionally attuned to be on the lookout for caring, or a lack thereof, and they seek out and thrive in places it is present. (Elias et al., p. 6)

These educators and scholars believe that "social and emotional development and the recognition of the relational nature of learning and change constitute an essential missing piece in our educational system" (p. 12). Their ideas are supported by the success of the program at the Valeska Hinton Center and what the cognitive neuroscientists and informed educators are telling us about the critical role of emotion in learning. In summary, Elias et al. (1997) write that

> Many elements of learning are relational (or, based on relationships), and social and emotional skills are essential for the successful development of thinking and learning activities. . . . Processes we had considered pure "thinking" are now seen as phenomena in which the cognitive and emotional aspects work synergistically. (p. 3)

If learning is grounded in emotions, then surely learning is best supported by leaders grounded in caring who influence and contribute to emotionally positive school environments through relationships embodying engrossment, action, and reciprocity.

Hart and Bredeson (1996) focus specifically on the type and levels of a principal's influence on learning, asserting that "principals make a difference in student achievement and school outcomes" (p. 211). They report less clarity about how that difference happens, but say that their review of the literature affirms "that the behaviors, beliefs, and symbolic leadership of principals have both direct and indirect impact on student learning" (p. 211). I agree with their statement that "it is difficult (and may be a futile exercise) to track the linkages between principals' leadership behaviors and student outcomes" (p. 211). Whether they can trace the linkage or not, whether the impact is direct or indirect, staff and parents believe that Hinton's caring leadership plays a role in enhancing learning. His behaviors and beliefs seem to be a clear illustration of Hart and Bredeson's (1996) conclusions that "principals influence student learning outcomes directly and indirectly by what they do, what they believe, and how they use symbols" (p. 219). My contention is that Hinton's influence on learning of students and teachers is both direct and indirect, begins with his own willingness to learn, and is multiplied through his commitment to caring relationships. His indirect influence on learning is through the teachers and the school environment, but he also cares directly. His direct caring for children is expressed through knowing their names; giving them undivided attention; expecting them to do their best; and giving them loving admonitions, words of praise, and hugs. His direct caring for teachers is expressed in personal support, professional encouragement, paying attention to their needs, giving time to securing resources, and respect.

Ultimately, the question of whether caring leadership can enhance learning is unanswerable in any definitive way. It raises the larger question of why any of us in education do what we do. Hinton's caring relationships with the staff, students, and their families are his motivation and the joy of his calling as an educator. Experiencing this joy completes a circle for him, strengthening him to persist in caring. On some days the children's hugs keep him going. He experiences joy when he can reach beyond the rules to make things better or to enhance the quality of life of a teacher, child, or parent. As a principal, he continues to see himself as both a learner and a teacher. "Early in my teaching career, my motivation became clear," Hinton said to me. "I do what I do because I want to enhance the growth of others and give back to those who helped me."

Hinton's "give back" brings to mind the words "giving forward," a concept developed by Lawrence-Lightfoot (1994) in the conclusion of a book profiling the personal and professional lives of six African Americans. One coined the phrase "giving forward" when speaking about her own motivation to achieve:

> My determination and obligation to do these things comes from my family first. I grew up in an extraordinary family that encouraged us to be the best we can be. . . . And I grew up receiving the gifts of neighbors, friends, and teachers whom you can never pay back. *All you can do is give forward.* (p. 477)

Lawrence-Lightfoot returns to this concept in the ending of the book, concluding about the six individuals, "Their lives are less focused on what they will acquire and more shaped by what they will leave behind. . . . For all of us, giving forward means journeying home" (pp. 599–600). These words also describe Hinton, who gives forward from the strong faith lived and learned in his Southtown home. His mother's caring lives on in his own compassion, nurturing the next generations. Hinton's caring seems grounded in wisdom from the deepest layer of Peoria's history, from the time when Native Americans fished and hunted in this area of central Illinois. Long ago and today, Native American grandmothers teach that every action should be considered in light of its impact on the next seven generations (Sams, 1993).

QUESTIONS FOR PERSONAL REFLECTION

How do I keep informed about research that has the potential to enhance students' learning?
What indicators of student learning do I value?
How do I show students in my school that I care about their learning?
What motivates my professional commitments?

◄§ 8 §►

Creating Caring Schools

> In recent years, school culture and climate have been popular topics in educational literature. . . . Two thematic threads running through much of this work in the area have important implications for administrators. The first of these is that the culture of a school has important and far-reaching effects on the thinking and actions of students and teachers. The second is that administrators can do much to shape, define, sustain, or change a school's culture. Leaders seeking to operate under a caring ethic surely would seek to cultivate a culture where such an ethic could flourish.
> —Lynn G. Beck, *Reclaiming Educational Administration*
> *as a Caring Profession*

As BECK SUCCINCTLY STATES in the introductory quote, school culture has an important influence on students and teachers; furthermore, leaders influence and can change a school's culture. Much of the writing about caring in schools focuses on caring in classrooms by teachers. However, some examples do exist of descriptions of caring school leadership and the challenges of developing a more caring total school culture or environment. The purpose of this chapter is to explore findings from these studies of caring elementary, middle, and high school principals and to relate discussion of the findings to Hinton's leadership. Four descriptions of caring school leadership are the result of single case studies, two of which the authors have written about more than once (Noblit, 1993b; Courtney & Noblit, 1994; Beck, 1994a; Beck & Newman, 1996; Dillard, 1995; Kratzer, 1996). Ryan and Friedlaender (1996) completed an extensive study of caring middle schools and comment in their report on the principals. Two questions provide focus for this chapter: How have other principals transformed existing school environments into more caring places? What are the challenges principals experience in building more caring school environments?

ELEMENTARY SCHOOLS

Kratzer (1996) and Courtney and Noblit (1994) address development of caring in elementary schools from different perspectives. Reporting on a year-long ethnographic study of one urban low-income school, Kratzer (1996) describes both cultural attributes and structural components of caring in the school. Courtney and Noblit (1994) frame a Southern elementary school principal's story through two lenses: Noddings's (1984) distinctions between authentic and aesthetic caring, and Fisher and Tronto's (1990) four phases of caring. They tell the story of a principal cultivating caring in a troubled setting. In a separate article, Noblit (1993b) analyzes the same school and leader to explore contradictions implicit in instituting caring in a school.

Jackson School, Los Angeles, CA

Kratzer (1996) profiles a Los Angeles school that she calls Jackson, an exceptional urban low-income, predominantly Latino elementary school, located 16 miles from downtown Los Angeles. A majority of the residents of this community are blue-collar workers or unskilled laborers. Many immigrant families from Latin America, Southeast Asia, and the Middle East live in this working- to lower-middle-class community. The school experiences a high turnover, with about 65% transient students. The majority of students, 92.6%, are Hispanic. Of the total of 1,170 students, 90% are eligible for Title I services, 76% are classified as Limited English Proficient, and 95% qualify for free or reduced-fee lunches and breakfasts. The school has a year-round schedule operated on three tracks due to overcrowding. The staff includes a principal, assistant principal, bilingual/Title I coordinator, full-time counselor, 2 special education teachers, and 40 regular education teachers.

Writing about this effective urban elementary school, Kratzer (1996) asserts that effective schools research "has not been able to ascertain how such schools develop" (p. 2). In her own research, Kratzer asks, "Has the school always been this way, or did it recently go through a major transformation, and, if so, what particular factors seem related to this transformation?" (p. 8). She reports that "research from a variety of disciplinary perspectives presents the argument that the best schools are places where a strong sense of community or 'family' exists" (p. 2).

Caring Leadership Practices. Kratzer (1996) comments on formal and informal manifestations of caring community. Formal restructuring of governance to a site-based management model, changes in hiring practices, and revamping the school schedule, as well as increased parent involvement, all contributed to a more participatory and empowering climate. The school's sense of itself as a caring community made these structures work; that is, the community gave the structures power. In Kratzer's words,

> While restructuring did not cause the sense of community, many of the structures that were put in place in the last few years helped to foster community by promoting interaction, collaboration, group problem-solving, dialogue, and a sense of ownership and empowerment. Conversely, that a strong sense of community existed at Jackson prior to restructuring helped provide a smooth transition into more participatory forms of governance. (p. 24)

Two specific structural changes helped foster community. The school instituted a committee process for the hiring of new teachers. The committee included several teachers, administrators, and the bilingual/Title I coordinator. The committee process, often remarked on by newly hired teachers, contributed to bonding of the new and old staff members. Committees looked for new personnel whose beliefs and teaching practices would fit with the school. A new scheduling of recess and lunch also fostered community. For 20 minutes over recess and 30 minutes over lunch, all teachers were free at the same time, except for the kindergarten and prekindergarten teachers (p. 22). Teachers engaged in collaborative planning as a result of scheduling for common planning time.

In exploring the link between achievement and caring, Kratzer (1996) describes several informal or cultural practices of caring by the school's administrators:

> They had no problem stepping in to cover a class if a teacher had an emergency. If a teacher needed to teach on a day his child was out of school, the administrative staff did not mind if the child came to Jackson with her parent for the day, spending the day in her parent's classroom or visiting in another room. This personal/professional crossover helped to solidify the feeling of family at the school. Teachers felt free to care for each other because they knew the administrators would support them as well. (p. 14)

Another informal manifestation of community at Jackson was that the teachers felt free to take action without waiting to ask an administrator for permission, a manifestation of autonomy or empowerment that Hinton also encourages. Site-based management facilitated the flexible enforcement of policies and rules. Parents said they always felt welcome at the school. The principal's office door, right next to the main entrance, was never closed. All had access to the principal and assistant principal, whether they were parents, teachers, students, classified staff, or outside visitors. Personal/

professional crossover or a breaking down of professional distance, modeling of interpersonal caring, and flexible enforcement of rules by Kratzer's unnamed principal further evolved the school as a caring community.

These informal caring leadership practices contributed to the good relationships existing between faculty and the administrators. Faculty expressed confidence in the administrators, the school, and each other in saying that they would want their own children to attend the school. Kratzer (1996) describes the relationship changes that accompanied the restructuring as being fundamentally about reciprocity, echoing a key component of caring as defined by Noddings (1984). Speaking of ways that relationships in the school had changed, for example, "administrators saw themselves as servants of both teachers and parents, going out of their way to provide resources for individuals in both groups, and looking for ways to help lessen the burdens and stresses of teaching and parenthood" (Kratzer, 1996, p. 30). In summary, "The development of community at Jackson occurred over many years, beginning with teacher relationships and the priority of creating a safe school environment, and spreading out to include all stakeholders and a myriad of instructional, climate and governance issues [citations omitted]" (Kratzer, 1996, p. 25). The process of becoming a more caring school may begin with formal restructuring, including site-based management, shared decision-making, and parent involvement. Facilitated by a prior sense of community, Jackson School's restructuring led to informal changes in all levels of interpersonal relationships. Relationships became more reciprocal and therefore more caring. Flexible enforcement of rules and policies as well as much personal/professional crossover or intermingling became norms. Finally, the more participatory approach to decision-making and problem-solving impacted instructional, climate, and governance issues.

Challenges to Caring Leadership. Kratzer's (1996) report clearly describes leadership practices that created a more caring community, but she is silent about the challenges. "The fact that the students and teachers are never all there at the same time, due to the year-round schedule" (p. 12), would seem to make a strong sense of community unlikely. Surely the 65% student turnover rate also provides a continuing challenge. Perhaps Kratzer does not focus on challenges of creating community because with site-based management the challenges seemed minimal:

> Jackson School is able to control 100 percent of its budget, make hiring and termination decisions (subject to contract and state regulations), adjust its yearly calendar and day-to-day schedule according to its needs, solicit external funding through grants and business partnerships, deal with the media

and other public entities as it sees fit, adopt its own curricula and textbooks, and provide professional development according to its needs and goals. (pp. 18–19)

Unlike many schools, Jackson School administrators and faculty apparently enjoy site-based management in its ideal form and have the power to make major decisions. Perhaps the freedom and power minimize the challenge of change by enhancing faculty ownership. This autonomy, according to Kratzer, along with a consensus approach to shared decision-making, has contributed greatly to the school's evolution as a caring community.

George Watts Elementary School

Watts School, the oldest school in Durham, North Carolina, was built in 1916, and as a result of school desegregation now serves families from two distinct neighborhoods. "One is the traditional neighborhood of white, upper-middle-class Trinity Park residents. The other is the working class, African-American neighborhood of Walltown" (Courtney & Noblit, 1994, p. 69). The school is 65% African American, with 300 students K–5. When Courtney was hired as principal of Watts in the mid-1980s, the school had replaced three principals in three years. He was hired specifically to bring unity and stability to the school through caring. In writing about Watts, Courtney and Noblit (1994) present "the case of a principal who tried to care and tried to bring caring into the language and culture of one school" (p. 68). Courtney and Noblit argue that relationships in a school, such as those a principal will have with students, faculty, and parents, ought to mix both *authentic* (reciprocal interpersonal relationships) and *aesthetic* (abstract commitment to ideas) caring (Noddings, 1984). To suggest possibilities for the mixture, they examine Courtney's work as principal of George Watts Elementary School. The intent of their examination is to expand the meaning of caring beyond authentic and aesthetic to include Fisher and Tronto's (1990) overlapping and intertwining phases of caring: *caring about, taking care of, caregiving,* and *care-receiving*. What did Courtney do to develop a more unified and caring school and what challenges did he encounter are questions the authors specifically address.

Caring Leadership Practices. Courtney and Noblit (1994) organize their discussion of caring leadership practices according to Fisher and Tronto's four phases of caring. To demonstrate that he *cared about* the school, Courtney tried to be visible in the community. He invited more participation at traditional faculty and PTA meetings. Courtney did not establish an initiative to change the school and the ways the teachers taught, but put the teachers in charge of setting goals and structuring their own staff develop-ment. He bolstered the improvement efforts through conversations, writ-ten notes, and staff luncheons. He featured teachers in press releases and professional publications. He reestablished rituals that had been lost, in-cluding singing the school song and having a mascot. Community assem-blies and award certificates "were celebratory markers that the school was being taken care of" (p. 76). Courtney was "visible in classrooms, avail-able to the children for conversations. He greeted them and bade them farewell each day" (p. 77), and took responsibility for getting resources and funding for new learning experiences for the students.

Courtney also began to heal the split in the school by reaching out to the Walltown community in a variety of ways. He created advisory boards, both internal and external, with representatives from both communities. He also did something unusual by inviting Noblit, a university professor known for his work on caring, to use Watts as a research site. This school/university collaboration proved to be most instrumental to the process of creating a more caring community. In its initial phase the collabora-tion evolved into an oral history project conducted by Noblit and uni-versity graduate students to reclaim the history of both communities served by the school. The residents of Walltown began to feel more in-cluded, and understood that the principal cared about their community, too, even though he was not African American.

Courtney and Noblit state that "the real activity of any school is con-sumed with the second phase of caring, the activities of *taking care of*. The day-to-day life in schools revolves around taking care of students and others" (1994, p. 73). They argue that this step requires making public a moral commitment to care. Courtney defined his role as *taking care of* teach-ers, and both informally and formally sought to find out what teachers needed and respond to these needs. Having done this, Courtney proceeded with a variety of initiatives, careful at each step to solicit input from the teachers. For example, he responded to teachers' requests for a stronger discipline policy by instituting a schoolwide approach. At the same time, he invited teachers to participate in a second collaboration with the uni-versity, the ethnographic study of caring in classrooms. This study served as Courtney's public moral commitment to caring, and became the vehicle for conversation about caring as a value. A Lilly Endowment grant sup-ported this study, which was designed to help teachers develop skills and knowledge to assist in their caregiving with students.

Moving to Fisher and Tronto's third phase, *caregiving*, Noddings's dis-tinction between aesthetic and authentic caring is dramatic, because "in traditional administrative logic, it is the principal's job to see that the teachers care for the students" (Courtney & Noblit, 1994, p. 77). They write,

"It should be clear that the teachers were primarily giving care to the students; Michael [Courtney] was primarily giving care to the teachers" (p. 79). Echoing Fisher and Tronto, Courtney and Noblit suggest that the responsibility of the principal is to facilitate caregiving for students by providing the variety of resources the teachers need in order to be caregivers.

Finally, Courtney and Noblit (1994) discuss *care-receiving* by teachers, by the two communities served by the school, and by the students. Based on what he perceived the teachers to value, Courtney used his position of authority to serve as a buffer between them and the central office. He mediated demands and responded to information requests himself rather than passing them on to the teachers. He stalemated requests for curriculum alignment that came from the district office, and he shared power with the advisory council, to give a few specific examples. In spite of the complication provided by his position of authority as the principal, however, "the teachers defined themselves as being cared for when the principal was 'doing something good for the children'" (p. 81). Additionally, Courtney and Noblit talk of how the children "happily identify him [Courtney] as their school principal, hug him, and so on. Here we can also see how much the teachers are giving care to him. They have constructed a shared belief among the children that he is a principal who cares about all of them" (p. 83); thus he also becomes a care-receiver.

Summarizing their blending and reinterpretation of the meanings of aesthetic and authentic caring, Courtney cared aesthetically by initiating a dialogue about caring. He used his power "to articulate caring as the purpose of the school and protected and supported the teachers as they embodied authentic caring" (Courtney & Noblit, 1994, p. 84). In so doing, Courtney went beyond what was officially required. His *caring about* students, parents, and two communities led him to find ways to *take care of* the teachers and to educate teachers about caring, but without abdicating taking care of the children to the teachers. His *caregiving* for the teachers enabled them to be better caregivers for the students. Courtney and Noblit conclude that when a principal is able to become a caregiver, too, then the bureaucratic limits on caring are changed. The cycle of caring was completed as the teachers, students, and even Courtney all understood themselves also to be *care-receivers*. Courtney has come to this new understanding of how to blend aesthetic and authentic caring:

> In his role he cares aesthetically. When caring about symbols, images, ideas and abstractions, the principal is negotiating the meaning of caring in the school. Clearly, he has authentic caring relationships with some of his teachers and some of the children and families, but his role limits the extent of this. His role is to set the context for caring, to pay attention to the more abstract

issues that surround developing caring relationships. This level of aesthetic caring is a necessity if teachers are to find authentic caring a significant part of their role. (Courtney & Noblit, 1994, p. 83)

Challenges to Caring Leadership. Writings by Courtney and Noblit (1994) and Noblit (1993b) more than make up for Kratzer's silence about challenges to caring in schools. Courtney and Noblit (1994) view the bureaucratic structure of schools as a major challenge to caring leadership. They write: "The key issue was whether the teachers and community would see his wishes [for the school to improve] as caring or as exercises of this authority. In retrospect, it is clear that they were perceived as both" (p. 80). Additionally, Courtney and Noblit view the bureaucratic structure as necessarily separating *caregiving* from *taking care of.* Furthermore, they recognize that an emphasis on higher test scores by those in upper levels of the district bureaucracy seems to render caring at a building level as less than consequential. They conclude that "the bureaucracy of schooling does distort caring to meet its needs and structure" (p. 84). All principals face the contradiction of caring and evaluation responsibilities. Courtney handled the inherent contradiction by closely supervising staff, but with an emphasis on coaching, setting goals, and providing professional development opportunities. He used the supervision and evaluation process to demonstrate care.

Courtney confronted racial challenges as a White Yankee dealing with what Noblit called the contradiction of desegregation. The uniting of two communities required tradeoffs, thus presenting the challenge of equity, as caring for one group often implies less than equal caring for another. Speaking of another kind of tradeoff, Courtney and Noblit state: "The responsibility to take care of all the participants in the school means that, by design, the principal's role is always structured by trade-offs—trade-offs in how much effort can be given to any one constituency, in how much one's caring for some may enhance or diminish the power to care for others, and in how much the principal's caring burdens the teachers" (1994, p. 77). Another of his challenges was what Noblit calls the contradiction of improvement—that to emphasize caring implies that faculty have not been sufficiently or properly caring: "Any effort on his [Courtney's] part to promote or even study caring carried with it an implication that his new faculty did not care enough about their students" (Noblit, 1993b, p. 7).

Finally, there is the challenge of the contradiction of success that calls good principals to new positions. Whereas Beck has argued that commitment is "an integral part of caring" (1994a, p. 199), Noblit (1993b) sees it as a source of potential contradiction. Courtney stayed at Watts only three years and then, because of a variety of pressures, chose to leave the school for a high school principalship that represented a more prestigious position. In effect, some perceived him to have used his success with caring to further his own career. Hinton has also struggled with this contradiction or challenge of success. The temptation to leave can come in many forms: the opportunity to earn more money, to relocate, or to affect a wider community, to name a few. From Hinton's perspective, a commitment over time is important, but maintaining the commitment is an area of challenge for any successful principal. His leaving Harrison to take the principalship of the new early childhood center was a decision he felt good about, but he wonders what he will choose to do in the future as other professional opportunities occur. I once asked Hinton directly what he would do if he were to get the Valeska Hinton Center where he wanted it. Would he stay around and enjoy the results or undertake a new challenge? He replied that he would probably want to go to another building somewhere and start the process all over again because he enjoys the challenge.

MIDDLE SCHOOLS

Ryan and Friedlaender (1996) describe schools that changed from bureaucratic organizations to families through implementation of a variety of reforms associated with an ethic of care that went against conventional paradigms. The schools initiated scheduling changes, invited parents to be partners, collaborated with social agencies, and shifted the focus from content-centered to child-centered teaching. Ryan and Friedlaender's report about middle schools "becoming caring" derives from a significant large-scale qualitative study supported in part by the Carnegie Corporation of New York. The schools they studied were guided by recommendations set forth in *Turning Points* (Task Force on Education of Young Adolescents, 1989), including the recommendation that one of the traits that schools seek to develop in young adolescents be "the capacity to care and act ethically" (p. 1).

In introductory paragraphs, Ryan and Friedlaender (1996) consider the question, "What is a caring school?" They cite Noddings's (1984, 1992) attention to caring as a relationship between two persons and also as a foundation for school reform. They believe that school culture influences teachers, and principals influence school culture. "Thus schools as well as individual teachers can be thought of as caring," they conclude (Ryan & Friedlaender, 1996, p. 3). The schools they studied worked toward becoming caring by emphasizing care at the community, organization, and classroom levels.

Caring Leadership Practices. To develop caring at the level of community, leaders of the schools studied by Ryan and Friedlaender (1996) created partnerships with parents and reached "beyond school yard boundaries for resources and assistance to meet students' non-academic needs and to broaden student learning opportunities" (p. 12). How did administrators contribute? "In several schools with non English-speaking parents, Spanish speaking administrators attempted to make the school more accessible by initiating contact with parents, and hiring Spanish-speaking parents to work in the office" (p. 10). According to Ryan and Friedlaender (1996), creating partnership relationships with parents required a reconceptualizing of roles. Parents were invited into the schools they studied in a variety of ways. Some invitations involved simple hospitality and creating a more welcoming environment for parents. Other invitations were for parents to participate in school decisions. Schools shared parenting information with parents and provided classes.

Reaching beyond the schoolyard boundaries often resulted in "initiating on-site health services or by facilitating community agencies' delivery of health services" (Ryan & Friedlaender, 1996, p. 12). Ryan and Friedlaender (1996) explain that as schools sought to structure educational and interpersonal relationships with school personnel and community members, a variety of things occurred, including teachers becoming more involved in children's lives as illustrated by inviting students to their homes for dinner. "Administrators, at one school, conducted home visits and called parents to increase attendance" (p. 13). "As one school administrator explained *school is not separate. . . . They're realizing that home, school, and community; it's all one. It's all part of their lives*" (p. 13).

Caring at the organizational level in the Ryan and Friedlaender (1996) study was accomplished, the authors report, through the following three types of activities: "establishing and maintaining caring interpersonal relationships; implementing schoolwide activities that demonstrated care for students and teachers; and adopting structures and norms that pressed teachers to address student needs and reconceptualize their professional roles" (p. 14). Administrators were key:

> Principals at many schools were credited with maintaining a child focus. Whether through hiring practices or by serving as examples, the principals at these schools set a tone on campus that permeated throughout the staff. In our poorest schools, staff understood that *the kids are made or broken* by their actions. (p. 15)

Although principals were important in the Ryan and Friedlaender study, "as one teacher commented, *we no longer look at our principal as the total leader-*

ship of this school. It's really up to all of us" (p. 15). Teachers took more responsibility for leadership, and communication between faculty and principals was open and enhanced. Ryan and Friedlaender describe programs to enhance the self-esteem of students by giving them responsibility and treating them with respect. For example,

> [o]ne principal, who utilized low achieving students to work in the front office, explained, *we recruit our office aides very intentionally and purposefully to reflect the ethnic make-up of our building. . . . I'm working to improve the children's self-concept—to show them they can be successful.* (p. 16)

In the Ryan and Friedlaender study, structures developed to foster closer teacher–student relationships included teaming, advisory programs, and other collaborative arrangements. At several schools administrators were "credited with creating an environment supportive of risk taking, one that made change safer for teachers" (p. 19).

Finally, administrators encouraged changes at the classroom level. The challenge was for teachers to move from traditional classroom practices, guided by what Ryan and Friedlaender (1996) call an ethic of service, to behaviors motivated by an ethic of care. Administrators supported teachers in the creation of more responsive classroom environments. Many teachers believed that genuine caring involved helping students help themselves. Classroom practices initiated to promote caring included dialogue about teen issues and real-life experiences, making connections across subjects, using cooperative learning, and bringing other adults into the classroom.

In concluding their analysis, Ryan and Friedlaender (1996) suggest that middle schools guided by an ethic of care emphasize human growth and becoming, empathy, responsibility, and continuity (pp. 3–4). These constructs also describe the Valeska Hinton Center. To summarize, the focus on *human growth* recognizes student achievement or cognitive growth as only one component, also including concern for emotional, physical, and social growth. Schools with *empathy* are places where persons have an understanding of the "circumstances that shape students' lives and conditions in their communities" (p. 4) and do not see their mission as "fixing" the student or community. *Responsibility* is used to suggest the responding that follows understanding. And *continuity* is used in the sense of belonging that both adults and students experience in a caring school.

Challenges to Caring Leadership. Ryan and Friedlaender's (1996) study of caring middle schools concludes with a section on confronting the challenges to care. They write:

In their efforts to become more caring, our schools encountered a number of tensions. These tensions occurred because the steps taken by our schools to implement a school program, guided by an ethic of care, conflicted with traditional notions of schooling, shaped by an ethic of service. (p. 23)

Specifically, the tensions revolved around scheduling difficulties, limited time and financial resources, lack of agreement about the proper role of the school, and political struggles to shape a school's direction (p. 23). Scheduling tensions included problems of finding time for parent and community collaboration. Budget cuts and limited resources affected programs directly through personnel cuts. In addition, because district priorities were not focused on caring, financial difficulties occurred. Sometimes resource cuts underlined how decision-makers at the district and state levels limit autonomy at the building level. Parents and teachers resisted some schools' caring reforms by pressuring for accountability framed as test score success. Teachers resisted role redefinition, particularly the redefinition of parents as partners, and the involvement of health and social service agencies in the schools. Struggles ensued between those who believed in child-centered versus content-centered teaching, and conflicts arose between teacher and student needs. Political tensions centered on power because "changing the relationships between schools and communities, teachers and parents, teachers and administrators, teachers and their colleagues, and teachers and students challenged conventional notions of schooling and became fertile ground for confrontation" (p. 27). Confronting these political tensions required principals to stay focused and be articulate. The authors conclude: "By challenging the conventions prescribed by an ethic of service, our schools made great strides toward becoming caring" (p. 31). The historical reality is that middle schools as bureaucratic institutions operate from an ethic of service, a difficult perspective to change. However, the authors report that change did happen.

SECONDARY SCHOOLS

Dillard (1995) and Beck (1994a) have each developed portraits of caring female high school principals. Dillard grounds her portrait of an African American principal in issues of race and gender, stating that one of the purposes of the portrait is to transform "our current conceptualizations of what leadership is and what leadership means" (p. 543). Beck, on the other hand, clearly focuses on caring, seeking to discover characteristics of Wilson High School that contributed to its caring reputation, as well as to discover the ways in which the principal was contributing to the school's evolution.

Rosefield High School

Dillard (1995) profiles a school she calls Rosefield High School, described as situated in a metropolitan city in the northwestern United States. Mandatory districtwide desegregation transformed Rosefield between 1982 and 1990 from a nearly all-White school of 1,600 to a predominately Asian, African American, and Latino/Hispanic student body of 800. The previous principal, a White male, was transferred to a suburban school in the second year following desegregation when the board appointed Gloria Natham to her first principalship. Previously, she had been a history teacher, multiethnic curriculum coordinator, and vice principal, all within the same school district. Commenting on her appointment, Natham said, "'I was brought here to clean up this mess and relate to these kids'" (in Dillard, 1995, p. 545). She came into a school perceived to have gone downhill with the arrival of large numbers of non-White students. As Natham put it,

> "When I came to Rosefield, the kids weren't in class. They were walking the halls. And almost every kid walking the halls were Black and Hispanic kids. They'd still be there happy as clams if we didn't get after them and the teachers whose class they were suppose [sic] to be in." (in Dillard, 1995, p. 557)

Dillard explores Natham's leadership through the principal's heritage as an African American, a woman, and a Catholic. The analysis is presented explicitly as a reaction to the effective schools literature and its antiseptic noncontextual portrayal of effective leadership in urban schools. Dillard asks the reader to be aware that both the researcher and the researched are African American women.

Caring Leadership Practices. Dillard (1995) describes Natham as a principal who modeled caring for students in culturally meaningful ways, calling Natham's (re)interpretation of leadership "talking back." Talking back involves going against the norms by articulating high expectations for students and holding teachers accountable for having high expectations. She shares several examples of how Natham "talks back," literally and also in her interpretation of the principal's role. One form of her talking back was to be "standing right in their faces" (p. 557), the faces of some of the more traditional White teachers who were content to have low expectations for the behavior and achievement of the Black and Hispanic students. She insisted that teachers have high expectations for all students even when her insistence resulted in grievances from the union. Natham decided to teach one course each semester, initially as a way to protest the inferior teaching candidates sent by the central office to Rosefield for interviews, but she continued to teach in order to reinterpret the role. Dillard views Natham's choosing to teach as a major (re)interpretation of the role of a principal. Finally, although an appointment to be principal of Rosefield might have been seen as undesirable, Natham refused that interpretation, instead seizing the opportunity to live out what she described as her moral obligation "'to be a part of the lives of our kids'" (in Dillard, 1995, p. 550) in a significant way.

Leadership as authentication means to Dillard that Natham consciously and deliberately nurtures and protects the children. Dillard (1995) offers the following observation:

> Nurturing and protecting children for African Americans hails from a history of communal responsibility for African children, for that matter, all children, often extending beyond blood kinship ties. . . . Given the changing community context at Rosefield, Natham sees a lack of real nurturing and caring for African American children that, although readily available to her while growing up, is not so readily available for today's children. (p. 551)

Filling that perceived void, Natham considers students to be like her own children, an attitude that echoes Hinton's. According to Dillard, this deeply personal commitment contributes to Natham's leadership as authentication, defined as nurturing and protecting our children.

Authentication also involves establishing credibility with parents and enlisting them to support student achievement. Natham protects and nurtures both the parent's ability and the child's ability to succeed in school by having high expectations. She is serious about her commitment. Her tone with parents and students is authoritarian. She communicates both praise and admonishments one-on-one, never embarrassing or ridiculing. She seeks out and nurtures relationships with students to foster their growth and achievement. In Dillard's (1995) words, "She is into the process of constructing relationships that enable self-empowerment for those in her care" (p. 553). Dillard writes, "Natham appears vigilant, supportive, and authoritarian, particularly with Rosefield's black parents" (p. 552). However, Natham established her authority and credibility with the parents, according to Dillard, through culturally meaningful interactions based on both her position as the principal and her capacity to create meaningful personal relationships. She has "direct, clear rules and expectations" (p. 554) and is known for "doing what is fair and serving as an advocate for students" (p. 555). Dillard also describes how "helping to create the ways and means for students to achieve was key to Natham's work as school principal" (p. 552). To promote achievement, Natham habitually goes through all 800 of the students' report cards and writes personal notes, using special stamps to recognize achievement and improvement.

Challenges to Caring Leadership. Dillard (1995) emphasizes several challenges to caring leadership, including racism and faculty not committed to integration or to meeting the needs of all students. Some 80% of the Rosefield faculty had not supported the integration of the school, and in the words of a younger African American teacher hired by Natham, "'Lots of people have been here at Rosefield for 25 to 30 years. They are community-tied. They have traditional ideas. The tend to be racist, but very subtle'" (p. 555). Natham does not have an open-door policy, explaining that she has "better things to do" with her time than constantly interact with teachers unless that interaction is directly related to the promotion of student achievement. She will intervene with teachers for two reasons: to mentor and support those who think similarly about "equality, fairness, and respecting and fostering cultural pluralism" (p. 556), and to discipline those suspected of a lack of effort or inequity in their work with students. "Natham maintains an underlying tone of social distance with most teachers" (p. 556).

Dillard (1995) describes Natham as an example, particularly for African American students: "She nurtures—and leads—by her presence, by her example, by the way she conducts her life and work in 'putting herself on the line for them'" (p. 557). Natham's student focus is similar to Hinton's. He often says, "We will do what is best for the children." Natham's words to the same effect are, "'If it's not good for kids, it's not good for Rosefield'" (in Dillard, 1995, p. 556). The article concludes with a meaningful statement of what Dillard calls two effective tenets of leadership in diverse ethnic and cultural settings: that leaders understand the salience of their own personal biography and understand "that concern, care, and advocacy for the individual needs of students is critical" (p. 559). Dillard writes that Natham's

> caring for students and interacting in communities in culturally meaningful and relevant ways is key. We have much to learn from the ways in which Natham (re)created an environment of care for students and the ways in which, given the limitations of the institution, she courageously and effectively used her own power and authority to do so. (pp. 559–560)

Many of the parents did not understand the importance of their children being in school or of education. Natham's leadership style was extremely effective with the African American and Hispanic students and their parents. Perhaps she could have been even more successful in creating an environment of care if she had been willing to abandon social distance and extend interpersonal caring to faculty who appeared not to be coming along with her beliefs. Perhaps not, however, because "for Natham, doing what is fair and serving as an advocate for students often puts her at odds with teachers" (p. 555), a reality fundamentally different from Hinton's. Whereas Hinton has not interpreted caring for children to be about race, Dillard sees Natham's commitment as a reflection of her heritage as an African American woman. When specifically asked whether his caring for children might be a reflection of his African American culture, Hinton replied, "Love has no color. All cultures value children." On the other hand, perhaps what Dillard says about caring for all children being a cultural value in the African American community illuminates Hinton's deep commitment to children. In his home all children were welcome, both Whites and African Americans. His parents frequently offered a place of hospitality and safety to struggling young people. Their example of caring for persons in need influenced Hinton's values.

Wilson High School

Beck (1994a) uses fictionalized names in recounting how a principal she calls Mary Story transformed a high school in the most economically depressed area of Los Angeles into a caring school community. Beck describes the school as a place where teachers and administrators put in long hours and work to serve families and students. She calls it a "safe, healthy community where persons are respected, supported, and encouraged to learn and grow" (p. 178). One of Beck's purposes was to identify characteristics of the school that contributed to its caring. She also wanted to discover the ways in which the principal specifically was contributing to the transformation of the school. Finally, she looked for theories to explain the relationships existing "among the principal's beliefs, activities, decision-making strategies, policies, and preferred organizational structures and the presence of a caring supportive school culture" (p. 179).

Caring Leadership Practices. Beck (1994a) describes a principal who transformed a school from a time bomb into a safe and good place. A strong base of parent support was important to the process. Beck identified the following as characteristics of the school that contributed to caring: a sense of safety through ownership; a belief that each person in the school was worthy of respect and deserving of empowerment and a voice; and an attitude of acceptance with adults at the school, while holding high standards, encouraging growth, and helping students deal with many less than ideal situations. Each of these are also characteristics of the Valeska Hinton Center, suggesting that a caring early childhood center and a caring high school have much in common. Beck suggests that the principal contributed to the transformation of the school into a caring community because she "embraced the complexity of the situation in which she found herself, surfaced conflict and handled it constructively, and evidenced a long-term commitment to the Wilson community" (1994a, p. 190).

Embracing complexity involves comfort with diversity, or as Beck (1994a) puts it, "cultures characterized by nurturing, supportive, interdependent relationships recognize and delight in the complexity of persons. Differences in beliefs, attitudes, preferences, and commitments are respected, encouraged, and viewed as contributing to the community" (p. 191). Another type of complexity was programmatic and budgetary. Story was good at finding resources, and seemingly unruffled by the multiplicity of the program offerings. Hinton has been extraordinarily successful at fund-raising and coordinates a complex array of program offerings for students, families, and others in the community. Interestingly, each principal has been successful in establishing and maintaining an on-site health clinic. Both of these principals seem to embrace complexity rather than "reduce complex, multifaceted activities and tasks to simple, linear, cause-and-effect phenomena" (p. 190). Story's comfort with conflict demonstrates comfortable professional respect for her staff, willingness to empower them, and respect for consensus or the wisdom of the group. She modeled principles of productive conflict behaviors. Conflicts were not seen as problems or as something to be suppressed. Teachers also describe Hinton as a person who will bring conflicts out into the open. Viewing complexity and conflict as expected or natural empowers staff to approach the challenges of urban education positively.

Story viewed her long-term commitment as critical to what she had been able to accomplish. Having been principal of the school for seven years, she expressed that the first year was about knowing her way around and the next two years were hard. She did not begin to see a change in the system and the culture until around the fourth year. "'I've heard that it takes 5 to 7 years to turn a school around. I guess it's more like 10'" (Beck, 1994a, p. 198), she said. Her 7-year tenure and long working days had helped build the trust that made genuine change possible. Hinton's commitment to the community served by the center is to some degree lifelong, and like Story, his working days are long. He has expressed that it usually takes about three years before a teacher begins to trust that she/he will be personally and professionally supported, can disagree with him, and is free to take risks and grow professionally.

Challenges to Caring Leadership. Although Beck's (1994a) focus is not on the challenges confronted by Story, clearly the challenges were similar to two described by Dillard: racism and low expectations for students rooted in views about poverty and race. Story had to combat what she calls a deficiency view of students, district policies that demeaned students, the need to remove teachers who have given up and are no longer trying to teach, some parents who do not appear to care very much, and the complexity of keeping the large percentage of student parents in school.

SYNTHESIS: PRACTICES AND CHALLENGES
OF CARING LEADERSHIP

The review of case studies presented in this chapter suggests a variety of perspectives for viewing the leadership practices and processes by which schools may evolve into more caring environments. My synthesis of the leadership practices and challenges common to caring leadership is offered in the form of two lists. In each list I combine my words about Hinton with language from the other case studies reviewed to present a comprehensive summary.

Common Practices

The following list of common practices of caring leadership represents insights from my analysis of Hinton's leadership combined with insights from analysis of case study descriptions in this chapter of how principals at all levels have led schools to become more caring communities:

1. Articulating values that support caring
   a. Caring is important in and of itself.
   b. All persons deserve to be treated with respect and dignity.
   c. High expectations for learning and achievement are essential.
   d. Treat students as you would your own children.
2. Embracing and viewing positively the complexity of difficult situations
3. Bringing conflict to the surface for constructive handling
4. Creating participatory approaches to decision-making and problem-solving
5. Acknowledging and valuing the reality of diversity
6. Being flexible in interpreting and enforcing rules and policies
7. Restructuring to support caring and create community
8. Inviting partnership with parents in the education of their children
9. Modeling caring in culturally meaningful ways
10. Demonstrating commitment over time

Common Challenges

The following list of common challenges to caring leadership is my synthesis of insights from Hinton's leadership combined with insights from the case studies reviewed in this chapter. I encourage those who would create more caring school communities to reflect on the following common challenges to caring school leadership encountered in one form or another by principals at all levels:

1. Racism and its many ramifications
2. Low expectations and deficiency views of students associated with race and class
3. Resources of time and money
4. Parents who seem not to care
5. Transient student populations
6. Teachers who have quit trying
7. "Contradiction of improvement"—a concept implying that attention to caring indicates a lack of caring in the past
8. Contentiousness associated with any change process
9. Bureaucratic traditions, structures, and associated practices and policies that demean and objectify people
10. Role contradictions associated with the principalship
    a. Requirement to supervise and evaluate teachers
    b. Distortion of perception of sincerity of principal's caring because of position of power
    c. Expectation that success will result in movement up the hierarchy

These leadership practices and challenges combine with the six themes of Hinton's caring leadership to present a comprehensive picture of what has been written about caring leadership. The role of this chapter is to confound skeptics who would dismiss caring leadership at an early childhood center as natural there but irrelevant to other levels of schooling. Taken as a group, these stories suggest that caring leadership, with its many faces and many voices, can contribute to creating caring school environments at any level.

Common Costs

Hinton's caring leadership has been consistently effective in both a very old and a brand-new building, whether stepping into an existing environment or starting from scratch. The purpose and meaning of Hinton's professional life is caring, a caring committed to helping others grow into their full potential. Hinton is also committed to an ethic of care. For him caring is not just a feeling, but is about the right of people to have their essence respected. Caring, for Hinton, is clearly both a value and a process, a way of being in relationships. He understands, however, why some administrators who care might be content to articulate caring as a value while at the same time choosing social distance or disengagement. He believes that for some administrators, whether it is conscious or subconscious, there is a "decision about how involved I am going to be, what price am I willing to pay if I care and am being caring." In other words, "some administrators are not willing to pay the psychological prices." He gave the following examples of price:

> The loss of time with your own family, never being done, being torn between the conception of success for which you are striving and the complexity, gravity, and frequency of problems, never being away from the job, and the anxiety and stress when there is so much to be done, so much you should be doing.

When one cares, self-esteem is oddly at risk, Hinton explained: "In fact, if you care, you start wondering if you are successful." As our discussion concluded, he mused, "The hurt of it all may be why some are not willing to invest in more personal relationships. My foundation, however, is in seeing that the quality of lives are improved and that successful and meaningful personal relationships are established."

QUESTIONS FOR PERSONAL REFLECTION

Which practices of caring leadership are common for me, and which do I find challenging?
Am I personally challenged by any of the common challenges to caring leadership?
To what extent can a principal afford to care?
Is the principalship my calling?

9

Leadership for a New Century

> We know at a common sense and experiential level that relationships matter a great deal, especially during times of intense change. We write about collaborative work attitudes and professional learning communities, but it is too easy for these to become abstract phrases. Once again, I believe that if we dig deeper into roles of emotion and hope in interpersonal relationships, we will gain a lasting understanding of how to deal with change more constructively.
>
> —Michael Fullan, "Emotion and Hope: Constructive Concepts for Complex Times"

In Kenneth H. Hinton, the mind of a nonconformist, a heart of compassion, and the eye of a builder combine in uncommon caring. Flexible and innovative, he has been extraordinarily successful with leadership of change. Fullan's (1997) words suggest why. These are complex times. Relationships matter. Emotion and hope foster collaborative work attitudes and nurture professional learning communities. Regrounding education in caring can give us excellent and equitable schools whose graduates are competent and caring. In this chapter I advocate that we educators go about the business of regrounding our educational system in care. Acknowledging complexity, I explore the barriers to leadership grounded in caring before elaborating on the hopeful possibilities: enhancement of learning, rebuilding of community, and reforging of justice. Finally, I return to Hinton's story and caring as a personal path.

A NEW METAPHOR

Beck and Murphy (1993), in a history of the principalship, examine what they call emerging metaphors for principals in the 1990s. One of the metaphors is "principal as person in the community" (p. 194). In elaborating the possible implications of this metaphor, Beck and Murphy write, "Leadership in the 1990s must continually bear in mind the reality that, regardless of differences in role, status, or achievements, all involved in schooling are equal in their personhood" (p. 194). They emphasize the importance of viewing schools as communities. "Recognizing that communities and their occupants flourish in caring, nurturing environments, these principals will seek to utilize a caring ethic to guide their decisions and their actions" (p. 195). Furthermore, Beck and Murphy see principals as people who will "celebrate the knowledge that they are persons who share vital, creative, caring relationships with others" (p. 195). This metaphor and others—principal as leader, as servant, as organizational architect, as social architect, as educator, as moral agent—are meaningful for what Beck and Murphy call an "all-encompassing challenge for principals in the 1990s . . . to lead the transition from the bureaucratic model of schooling, with its emphasis on minimal levels of education for many, to a post-industrial model, with the goal of educating all youngsters well" (p. 190). Beck, Murphy, and others seem to have been unduly optimistic in suggesting that this transition from the bureaucratic model might be accomplished in a decade, but surely there will be enough time in the new century. Perhaps we need a new metaphor.

Metaphors and definitions of leadership coexisting in our culture both influence and confuse. Leaders are still considered by many to be the dominant larger-than-life heroes who accomplish something significant, legendary, or new. Historically, leadership has also been considered "a social-influence process in which individuals get others to engage in activity or work" (Drath & Palus, 1994, p. 13). Drath and Palus clarify how these understandings overlap:

> [We] have not replaced the dominance construct with the influence construct. We have more likely supplemented dominance with influence. Influence as a way of understanding leadership is layered over with dominance as a way of understanding leadership. . . . More recently, a new layer, a new way of understanding leadership has been added: *participative leadership*, it might be termed. (p. 24)

Sharing their research, Bolman and Deal (1997) have a different angle. "Beyond vision, the ability to communicate the vision with passion, and the capacity to inspire trust, consensus [about leadership] breaks down" (p. 298), they write.

This portrait of Hinton offers a new metaphor: *the leader grounded in caring*. The metaphor carries its own vision and skills. Caring both is and gives purpose, transforms passion into actions, and builds relationships of trust. A leader grounded in caring concentrates on meaning-making (Drath & Palus, 1994), leads without easy answers (Heifetz, 1994), and offers self and spirit (Bolman & Deal, 1995). Critical to the waning of bureaucratic schools will be principals like Hinton who ground all decisions in caring, who care enough to do things differently, who embrace the potential inconsistency of flexibility, and who put themselves at risk for the sake of their students. How would communities and schools be different if leaders were grounded in caring? What if caring in schools were to become commonplace? What if departments of educational leadership emphasized that now, more than ever, those who would lead schools must be grounded in caring? What if caring were to become leadership's common ground?

LAYERS OF COMPLEXITY

Noblit (1993b) writes of caring's contradictions; Ryan and Friedlaender (1996) identify caring's tensions; I prefer to speak of caring's complexities. Contradictions pose traps that catch us, tensions fill us with anxieties, but complexity is simply the challenge of reality in the 21st century. "Is there still room for caring school leadership?" Blount (1996) asks in an analysis of the careers of exemplary female superintendents in the early decades of the 20th century. Her analysis offers historical perspective on the barriers to leadership grounded in caring. Blount profiles three early superintendents who demonstrated the importance of relationships with teachers, relationships with the community, concern for students, and flexible decision-making. These caring leaders were Ella Flagg Young, superintendent of the Chicago schools from 1909 to 1915 except for a brief break in 1913, Julia Richman, district superintendent in the New York City schools from 1889 to 1912, and Susan Dorsey, superintendent of the Los Angeles city schools from 1920 to 1929. Although successful superintendents, their caring leadership styles did not spread among other urban superintendents. Instead, the beliefs of the Department of Superintendence of the National Education Association (NEA) became prominent over time. "Finally, the department's insistence on standardization led many school systems to adopt common administrative practices [citation omitted] that left little room for the flexibility needed to build and maintain caring relationships" (1996, p. 24), Blount reports. Caring leadership is constrained by a host of historical, cultural, and personal complexities. I choose to address only two: the constraints of gender and bureaucracy.

Barriers of Gender

Cultural prescriptions for how to be male or female and perceptions that caring is a woman's way of leading are gender barriers to a widespread renewed emphasis on school leadership grounded in caring. As shown in Blount's (1996) profiles, a basic organizing concept of our culture is that women are subordinate to men, that leadership is a male domain. As Blount's (1996) historical account makes clear, the male superintendents' insistence on standardization prevailed over the female superintendents' ways of leading. At the level of the principalship, nurturing has been accepted and expected from women (Shakeshaft, 1987). Some women principals, however, believe that to be overtly caring as a leader, even to be too participatory, is to invite accusations of incompetence. Women are still a minority in school leadership positions. The subtle pressures of tokenism can cause a woman principal to be directive instead of nurturing in an attempt to fit in with the prevailing norms. Generally, authoritarian leadership from women is not well accepted. There are, of course, exceptions like Dillard's (1995) Gloria Natham, whose authoritarian stance was accepted as expressive of her care for minority students in need of her strong advocacy.

Gender barriers to caring by male principals are widely recognized. Because in our culture men are expected to have the answers, to be in control, many men learn to be stereotypically strong, decisive, and silent about their feelings. Emotions are considered out of place in the workplace. Hinton shared an example of a principal with whom he had worked as an administrative assistant. The man cared deeply, but presented a gruff exterior. He was not able to verbalize caring, perhaps because no one had articulated to him that this was acceptable for a man, Hinton believes. Hugging children was not in his repertoire, but behind the scenes he cared fiercely. "Some inner-city principals, like this man for whom I worked, are successful coming from a more authoritarian stance because people know that they do care," Hinton said. Anyone evaluating this principal's depth of caring for children based on his external public behaviors would have been mistaken. When principals follow gender stereotypes their caring is sometimes masked from others, and can even be hidden from themselves. Culturally prescribed gender expectations can be a barrier to overtly caring school leadership for women and men, but for different reasons. Confronting the gender barrier requires flexibility and a level of comfort with nonconformity.

Barriers of Bureaucracy

A crisis of community exists in America, wrote Bellah, Madsen, Sullivan, Swidler, and Tipton (1985) in a book that portrays habits of the hearts of representative Americans in the early 1980s. The crisis has not subsided. Our bureaucratic institutions are in need of being humanized in order to carry out their missions of care. "The need for care in our present culture is acute" (1992, p. xi), Noddings writes. She continues:

> Patients feel uncared for in our medical system; clients feel uncared for in our welfare system; old people feel uncared for in the facilities provided for them; and children, especially adolescents, feel uncared for in schools. Not only is the need for caregiving great and rapidly growing, but the need for that special relation—caring—is felt most acutely. (1992, p. xi)

In education, the dehumanizing bureaucratic evolution of traditional school administration (Blount, 1996) has influenced both the principalship and the superintendency, from my perspective, with at least three constraints to caring.

First, bureaucracy promotes inflexible enforcement of policies and rules. Noddings (1984) offers an example of uncaring, inflexible bureaucratic treatment when she recounts how school counselors and administrators treated patronizingly a parent who requested that a child skip a grade. The student had made unusual academic progress during two serious illnesses when, confined to bed, she had progressed well beyond her grade placement. Refusing to budge, those in charge told the parents that "all professional people want to push their children," illustrating how school professionals can treat people as types or cases rather than as persons. Noddings (1984) writes emphatically:

> The fact is that many of us have been reduced to cases by the very machinery that has been instituted to care for us. It is not easy for one entrusted with a helping function to care. A difference of status and the authorization to help prevent an equal meeting between helper and the one helped. (p. 66)

Blount (1996) also argues that "problems of rigid administrative structures and normalized practice hinder, if not prevent caring school leadership" (p. 28).

Operating as a second constraint on caring are bureaucratic responsibilities that reinforce the power rather than the personhood of the principal. The traditional power of the principalship is a structural and cultural reality that complicates caring relationships. The concept of professional distance encouraged by hierarchical structures is in opposition to the reciprocity of caring. Hierarchy implies that some persons are more important than others and institutionalizes inequality of worth.

Finally, bureaucratic time pressures are a third constraint that can overwhelm the underlying caring that commonly motivates educators. Bureaucratic tasks imposed on a principal by a central office sometimes take away a principal's energy and time for caring. For example, Hinton once confessed during an interview that he was feeling pushed, to some degree, to be a more traditional principal. I asked what he meant. He answered,

> Traditional to me, in terms of the principalship, means being a
> principal who is not so much engaged in terms of human dynamics,
> parent teacher conferences, doing home visits, the extra things that
> we do. For lack of a better example, personally delivering the
> Christmas baskets, those kinds of things. I am bothered by being
> removed from the classrooms. I am under the pressure of time and I
> am being asked to put together a plan to address possible funding
> shortfalls. So having to be more traditional to me means basically
> not becoming so involved in your staff, students, and parents in
> terms of their personal well-being because of the time pressures
> associated with other responsibilities.

As a person in a middle management role, Hinton was expected to comply with directives from those with higher rank. The problem was not putting together the plan, but the time pressure associated with central office deadlines. To summarize, rational and bureaucratic models were created for purposes of efficiency, control, and depersonalization. Caring school environments, on the other hand, result from the interaction of caring in personal relationships and structures that support and allow for caring relationships to develop over time.

Confronting rigid practices requires flexibility, a spirit of nonconformity, and a willingness to reach beyond the rules. An ethic of critique questions the way things are (Starratt, 1991), with all bureaucratic and other organizational arrangements viewed from a nonconformist perspective as open to change. The premise is that changing organizational arrangements will make schools better able to serve society's needs instead of individuals' needs for power and control. The focus is on uncovering injustice or dehumanization concealed by well-meaning policies and rules. I do not disagree with the ethic of critique. However, while organizational arrangements can be changed, I do not expect that all forms of educational bureaucracy will disappear any time soon. Confronting the barrier of bureaucracy to caring leadership is not a simple one-time task. Ultimately, caring must work its way into even the most bureaucratic central offices and become a central office value and way of being in relationships. Only when caring is supported in the central office, in the principal's office, in the hallways and classrooms, on the playground, and in the cafeteria will all children, families, and teachers finally feel that schools care about them. When "we look in vain for a layer at which it begins or ends" (Noddings, in Beck, 1994b, p. x), then caring will have rehumanized bureaucracy.

LAYERS OF POSSIBILITY

If caring leadership is constrained by complexities, it is at least equally filled with possibilities. Many whose work has already been referred to see caring as one avenue toward significant reform (Kohn, 1991, 1996; Starratt, 1991, 1996; Noblit, 1993a, 1993b; Sergiovanni, 1991; Noddings, 1992; Beck, 1994a, 1994b; Quint, 1994; Dillard, 1995; Lipsitz, 1995; Epstein, 1995; Newburg, 1995; Rossi & Stringfield, 1995; Lewis, Schaps, & Watson, 1995; Kratzer, 1996; Ryan & Friedlaender, 1996; Marshall, Patterson, Rogers, & Steele, 1996). My focus is on three particular possibilities: caring leadership enhances learning, rebuilds community, and reforges justice.

Enhancing Learning

Noddings (1995) underlines the importance of caring to learning when she argues that we should want more from education than academic achievement, but that "we will not achieve even that meager success unless our children believe that they themselves are cared for and learn to care for others" (pp. 675–676). Elias et al. (1997) also state as their collective opinion that attaining true academic and personal success without social and emotional learning is not likely (p. 3), citing as evidence results of studies of effective middle schools. Caring leaders cognizant of current brain research about learning will have a broad perspective on learning. Ryan and Friedlaender (1996) emphasize that "rather than focusing narrowly on student achievement, schools that are caring places take a broader view of their role in students' development" (p. 3). They observe, as did Hinton, that when the focus is on care and creating community, the instructional practices of teachers change: There is more emphasis on authentic instruction and assessment, including thematic teaching and cooperative learning, with an integrated curriculum at the center (p. 22). These teaching practices match those advocated by experts on brain-based teaching and learning (Caine & Caine, 1991; Sylwester, 1995; Jensen, 1998).

As a "creative and capable pedagogue" (Beck, 1994b), Hinton focuses on the learning of teachers, contributing to the learning of children by enabling teachers to reach their full potential. Hinton empowers professional growth by "leaving doors open for people to develop their positions and not limiting them to old ways," said the lead teacher at the Valeska Hinton Center.

If belonging to a caring school community contributes to emotional states that enhance learning, then the impact of caring on learning is certainly not confined to a particular age group. Beck (1994a) and Dillard (1995) have both written eloquently about female inner-city high school principals whose caring leadership behaviors have much in common with Hinton's. Although neither study of caring leadership in high schools focuses on higher test scores as indicators of learning, both authors report that improved student behaviors demonstrate much valuable learning about being productive members of a community. Beck (1994b) argues that caring leadership can help schools meet the challenge of improving academic performance. Lawrence-Lightfoot (1983) writes about high schools that "unless the school environment feels safe and secure they will not be able to focus on matters of the mind" (p. 356). Kratzer (1996) writes that "a causal link has been established, at least at the high school level, between the psychological environment of the school and student motivation and achievement" (p. 6), citing several studies in support of that conclusion.

At Harrison Primary School and at the Valeska Hinton Center, Hinton has been able to work with faculty, students, and parents to create environments in which minority and low-income students thrive. He is motivated by his own beliefs about how caring affects learning and is cognizant of discoveries of the cognitive neuroscientists about emotion's effects on learning. Parents are also seen as important to the school community's success with student learning. Hinton does not focus on what some might see as the deficits of his students or their parents, but on their strengths and potential. In holding a positive perspective, Hinton's thinking aligns with the Urban Learner Framework developed by staff at Research for Better Schools, located in Philadelphia. Their approach to school reform refocuses on assets of the urban at-risk students rather than negative labeling and stereotypes (Williams & Newcombe, 1994). James Comer and others have also focused on the resilience of urban families instead of their perceived inadequacy or deficiency (Comer, Haynes, Joyner, & Ben-Avie, 1996). In summary, a leader grounded in caring enhances learning by honoring emotions and empowering teachers to change and grow; by contributing to safe and supportive environments for students, parents, and teachers; by caring personally about teachers, students, and their families; and by viewing everyone from a positive perspective. Caring enhances learning when schools become communities where everyone comes to learn.

Rebuilding Community

A school leader grounded in caring rebuilds community by drawing a larger circle, by including families in the circle of caring. The fundamental attitude facilitating community-building is reciprocity. At the heart of Hinton is the reality of an underlying attitude of reciprocity, illustrated in what has been said about how "He treats every person equally and with respect," and that "He does not limit himself or anyone else by or to a role." In an interview, Hinton commented implicitly on the importance of reciprocity to caring:

> Many teachers don't realize that children have something to offer, parents have something to offer them. . . . I have found that many teachers are reluctant to make home visits because they don't truly understand the purpose. In a lot of their minds it is "I am making a home visit to give information about the child, how he or she is doing in school" as opposed to I'm making a home visit to establish a relationship with the parents, let them know that we are doing this together. "I need a friend—You need a friend." You don't do that over the telephone. You don't do that through correspondence. There is a better way of meeting face to face. . . . We don't have to agree with each other. That may not ever take place. We do have to respect each other. We do have to know about each other . . . know that each of us have something to offer.

Knowing children by name, meeting with the parents, and encouraging that teachers' home visits be about forming relationships of partnership with parents all illustrate Hinton's understanding of the reciprocity necessary in caring relationships.

An attitude of reciprocity invites those most likely to be excluded into the circle and overcomes their feelings of not belonging with the experience of worthiness. It is not enough to say "I care"; caring must be offered through action in a way that honors the mutuality of the relationship. A uniqueness of the Valeska Hinton Center is the commitment to working in partnership with low-income and minority parents. Educators here understand that "the way schools care about children is reflected in the way schools care about the children's families" (Epstein, 1995, p. 701). As a result of the school's commitment to partnership with parents, the circle of community is enlarged, and parents as well as children grow in their understanding of caring and community. Said a teacher, "I know at least five families that have changed, the way they parent, think, their motivation, how they hold their heads up. If we can save five families, the souls involved in those families, that changes the world." Ultimately, the larger circle must include more than parents and neighborhoods, and extend to and include the whole community.

Reforging Justice

The relationship between care and justice is the subject of controversy, the tension between care and justice predating Gilligan. Nevertheless, Gilligan (1982) widened a separation between caring and justice by gendering them as ethical constructs, even while viewing them as interwoven. As if in response to those who see a gulf, Starratt (1991) argues that a larger ethic requires the interpenetration of the ethics of critique, justice, and caring. Starratt also hypothesizes that an ethic of caring helps resolve the contradictions of competing conceptions of justice. "Justice means taking care of one another," wrote sociologists Bellah, Madsen, Sullivan, Swidler, and Tipton (1991, p. 194). Their statement offers an example of how the concepts are infused into each other. Beck (1994b) puts caring "at the top of the values hierarchy" (p. 77), asserting that caring must inform and guide a number of other ethics that have a place in educational leadership. Publication of the *Journal for a Just and Caring Education* began in January 1995, with the editors stating as its mission "to develop the idea of schools as sanctuaries in a tumultuous world and to promote the right of all children to a just and caring education" (Curcio & First, 1995, p. 3). Killen (1996) interprets caring and justice to be two distinct conceptual frameworks that coexist and are integral to human development. Based on her research into actual school attendance office practices, Enomoto (1997) tentatively argues that "it is possible to reconcile rather than simply negotiate care and justice" (p. 369) by returning to caregiving as the goal of schools as institutions. Hinton said that he saw justice in terms of morality or spirituality, as "a right of the essence of a person to be respected."

The controversy about the relationship between caring and justice can be reformulated as the proverbial question, "Which comes first? The chicken (caring) or the egg (justice)?" My answer is that caring comes first, has ontological rather than hierarchical primacy. As a human activity, justice-making is forged or fired by the passion of caring. Caring clearly precedes justice; justice is born from caring. The order is not usually reversed. When we care, we act, become angry with injustice and seek remedies. School leaders grounded in caring may pursue justice down many different paths. Do we concern ourselves with students' rights or their responsibilities? Do we focus on implementing the rules or on changing them to better serve the growth and development of young persons? Are we as individuals and a country more interested in procedural, distributive, or substantive justice (Bellah et al., 1985)?

Retrace any path of justice and one discovers caring as its source. The road to procedural justice leads to reexamination of the necessity and fair-

ness of policies, rules, and procedures, to questions about procedural practices that oppose principles of caring. On the road to distributive justice
we may meet Kozol (1991, 1995) and join caring's crusade for equity in
school funding, or the larger cause of conscience in the face of the unjust
distribution of wealth in our society. Searching for substantive justice, we
walk with Bellah et al. (1985, 1991), Beck (1994b), Quint (1994), Apple (1996),
Comer et al. (1996), Eaker-Rich and Van Galen (1996), Sergiovanni (1996),
Starratt (1996), and countless others who are wrestling with the larger
questions of justice and community. Renewed commitment to substantive
justice running throughout the institutional order of society could reforge
justice from caring and revitalize our country and its schools.

The building of the Valeska Hinton Early Childhood Education Center in the heart of Southtown represents the promise and possibility of justice reforged. Its section of Southtown lay barren, a virtual ghost town, until
the city and school district worked together to birth the new school envisioned for Southtown 15 years earlier. The leadership of a superintendent
who cared about equal opportunity called forth this unprecedented collaboration among bureaucracies. Peoria as a community has settled for
nominal integration, with every school in the district having at least a 20
percent minority enrollment achieved through busing of minority students
to predominantly White schools. Cross-busing, transporting White students
into predominantly minority inner-city schools, was never called for in the
district's desegregation plan. Ironically, the Valeska Hinton Center has been
popular with middle and upper-class families from across Peoria who value
its diversity, recognize its excellent educational program, and want their
children to experience its uniquely caring environment. Anchoring the
rebuilding of Southtown, the school has served as a racially integrated
center for a reemerging circle of neighborhood and community.

CARING: A PERSONAL PATH

Caring is always a personal path, crowded by complexity, unfolding into
possibility. My portrait of Ken Hinton has a four-sided frame. Caring as
purpose and meaning (Mayeroff, 1971), the bottom edge of the frame, has
grounded his teaching and his leadership and serves as his foundation. On
one side of the frame, I envision caring as an ethical orientation (Gilligan,
1982) with deep spiritual roots in home and church that guide his actions
and his decisions. On the frame's other side, I see caring as process, as a
way of being in relationships (Noddings, 1984) that springs naturally from
his heart. The label across the top of the frame reads, "A leader who makes
a difference." In a real sense, however, Hinton is not captured in the por-

trait nor contained within the frame. The book's portrait is not static; rather, the chapters' images are overlapping, forming a series of drawings even if the subject refuses to remain still.

> The present is the object of vision, and what I see before me at any given second is a full field of color-patches scattered just so. The configuration will never be repeated. Living is moving; time is a live creek bearing changing lights. (Dillard, 1974, p. 82)

The present is an ever-changing canvas through which caring unfolds a personal path. Nearing completion of six years as principal of the Valeska Hinton Center, Hinton was increasingly concerned about educational issues throughout the district, issues that were beyond his reach from the building level. A transition in the district's superintendency offered a change of path. John Garrett became interim superintendent on July 1, 1998, and was named superintendent in December. Responding with mixed emotions to a call from the larger community, Hinton accepted on July 1 Garrett's appointment of him to the newly created position of Assistant Superintendent for Community Programs. The newspaper headline called Hinton "a proven product": "Hinton, 51, will have many responsibilities including overseeing early childhood programs and the Valeska Hinton Center, working with family literacy and the adult education programs and supervising Title I funds, grants and the district's pilot health care program" (Brown, 1998a, p. A11). A subsequent article reported:

> Recently named District 150 assistant superintendent for community programs, Hinton will take his expertise districtwide, helping students, families and community members become lifelong learners. "My focus will be to make this a community of learners. Children cannot succeed without the community," Hinton said. "Mom and dad have to get it started and sometimes they need help." . . . "My purpose is to serve and to see to it that the children and the family get what they need," Hinton said. "I am very excited to be in this job." (Brown, 1998b, p. A18)

The reporter also wrote that "people describe Hinton, 51, as soft-spoken but firm; a good family man and a wonderful teacher and mentor" (Brown, 1998b, p. A18). An editorial writer, calling Hinton a kids-first appointment, wrote, "Over 30 years he has distinguished himself in virtually every position in which he's served. He is one of the hardest working, most committed, charismatic, kids-first administrators we know" ("Hinton," 1998, p. A4).

Hinton is also an appointment for justice. Some viewed Garrett's offer to Hinton as a response to the African American community's insistence that someone from their community represent them as an assistant superintendent. The story of how Hinton's appointment happened is not important. What does matter is that a homegrown Southtown principal has moved out of the valley and into the Central Office. Community historians will record that Hinton is the first African American who grew up in Peoria to serve at the assistant superintendent level. When a reporter addressed the issue of race directly with Hinton, he replied,

> "It so happens, I am an African-American and I understand what it means to be a minority and a male minority and I speak up, because in our society, that needs to be done," Hinton said. "I plan to represent all people in a fair and equitable way and I would like to be considered good for the whole community," Hinton added. (Brown, 1998b, p. A18)

Garrett's appointment of Hinton brings hope for a new sensitivity to diversity, hope for a genuine spirit of integration, to transform a school district and community where race still has the potential to unsettle. Like his mother before him, Hinton is recognized as a healer, and ours is a community in continuing need of racial healing. Hinton has traveled up the hill and out of Southtown. The whole community has become his home. If caring is possible in the central office, if one person on a caring path can make a difference, then the inflexibility of a central office's habitual bureaucratic practices will blur as energies of good people refocus on serving the needs of children and families. What is moving onto the central office stage in this historic town of early vaudeville is not an act, but the person and will of a serious, caring man who is determined to make a difference. His eyes look into the future, contemplating how to build a larger caring community that will last over time. Manifesting, perhaps, the spirit of the area's Native American ancestors, he envisions a community cradling with care the children of today and the next seven generations. If caring plays in Peoria, it can play anywhere.

QUESTIONS FOR PERSONAL REFLECTION

What are my melodies—my life's recurring themes?
What is my uniqueness?
Have I, for whatever reason, tuned out any important aspects of who I am?
Is my leadership grounded in caring?
Am I moving on my own personal path as a leader who makes a difference?

Appendix

GPA DATA

At the end of the 1997–98 school year, grade information was compiled for 140 children who had graduated from the center and were in grades two, three, and four in the Peoria public schools. Grades were compiled for 44 second graders, 69 third graders, and 27 fourth graders. Grades were not available for children who left the center to attend private or parochial schools. Nine additional students had left the district for reasons unknown, and 11 had been retained in the previous grade. The students are described by the following demographics: 80.7% low-income, free or reduced-price lunch; 60.0% African American, 36.4% White, and 3.6% Hispanic; and 55.7% male and 44.3% female. Table A.1 displays the mean grade point averages (4.0 = A, 3.0 = B, 2.0 = C, 1.0 = D, 0 = F) by academic subject, conduct, and effort for the 140 students by grade level.

Grade data were analyzed for answers to four questions: For former Valeska Hinton Center students, do any mean GPA differences exist between boys and girls? Do any mean GPA differences exist between African Americans and Whites? Do any mean GPA differences exist in the sex-by-race interaction? Is there a relationship between academic achievement and parent involvement? The first three questions were answered by using a 2×2 between-subjects ANOVA. GPA was calculated using reading, spelling, language arts, and math grades. The five Hispanic students were removed from the sample, leaving an N of 135. There was a statistically significant difference ($F = 8.91, df = 1, p = .003$) between boys and girls, with girls having a higher mean GPA (3.04) than boys (2.71). No statistically significant mean GPA differences existed between African Americans and Whites ($F = 2.62, df = 1, p = .11$). Finally, the sex-by-race interaction did not yield statistically significant mean GPA differences ($F = 2.91, df = 1. p = .09$). These results suggest that for this group of children, no GPA differences exist between African American and White students who attended

Table A.1. Mean GPAs by Academic Subject, Conduct, and Effort for Former Valeska Hinton Center Students, 1997-98

Grade	Subject	N	Mean	SD
2nd Grade	Reading	44	2.98	.82
	Spelling	44	3.20	1.00
	Language Arts	44	2.95	.91
	Math	44	3.02	.85
	Conduct	44	3.23	.86
	Effort	44	3.14	.77
3rd Grade	Reading	69	2.54	1.11
	Spelling	69	2.88	1.11
	Language Arts	69	2.49	1.07
	Math	69	2.55	1.06
	Conduct	69	2.94	.94
	Effort	69	2.86	.90
4th Grade	Reading	27	2.89	.75
	Spelling	27	3.07	.96
	Language Arts	27	2.78	.80
	Math	27	2.48	.89
	Conduct	27	2.96	1.02
	Effort	27	2.81	.88

the Valeska Hinton Center, although girls do appear to be earning better grades than boys at this point in their educational careers.

The fourth question, whether parent involvement and academic achievement are related, was examined through the following procedures. First, academic achievement was defined as grades, with four measures available: reading, spelling, language arts, and math. Parent involvement for each child had been labeled as low, medium, or high by the children's Valeska Hinton Center first grade teachers. The correlational procedure used was the Spearman rank correlation coefficient, a commonly used nonparametric measure of correlation between two ordinal variables. Since four tests of correlation were run (SPSS), a correction for inflation in Type 1 error rate was used (Bonferroni). Analysis of the correlations between parent involvement and grades (GPA) revealed statistically significant relationships between parent involvement and spelling ($r_s = .25, p = .003$) and between parent involvement and language arts ($r_s = .32, p < .005$). These data may be interpreted to say that as the level of parent involvement increases, so does achievement in spelling and language arts.

LONGITUDINAL STUDY MODEL

At Hinton's request, Dr. Paul Holmes, Peoria public schools Director of Research, Evaluation, and Testing, has undertaken a longitudinal study of *Iowa Tests of Basic Skills* results of former Valeska Hinton Center students. The two questions driving the analysis are (1) Do any achievement test score differences exist between Valeska Hinton Center students and students in a control group? and (2) Do achievement test score gains of Valeska Hinton students last over time? Holmes completed both a cohort group analysis and grade level analysis of four sets of achievement test data from four groups of students. These groups in the 1997–98 academic year included the current Valeska Hinton Center first graders and former Valeska Hinton Center students who are now in second, third, and fourth grades in their neighborhood schools. The model for the analysis appears as Figure A.1.

The Valeska Hinton Center opened with a kindergarten program only in 1993–94. The preprimary programs were added in 1994–95, and new

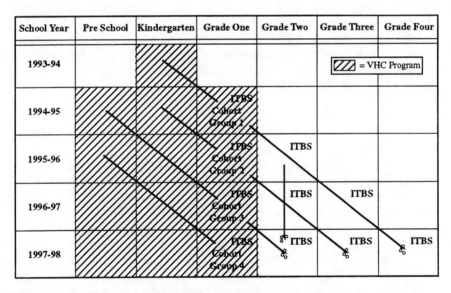

Figure A.1. Model for evaluating impact of Valeska Hinton Center program on academic achievement as measured by Iowa Tests of Basic Skills (ITBS). This model focuses on the academic growth of students as they progress from grade one to grade four (cohort group analysis), shown as diagonal lines, and differences in academic achievement across years at a single grade level (grade-level analysis), suggested by a vertical line. All analyses include a control group comprising students from another Title I school in the district. The ITBS is administered in early October.

kindergarten students joined the 1994–95 first graders in multiage primary classrooms. The first group of students to have been at the Valeska Hinton Center for two years entered second grade in their neighborhood schools in the 1995–96 academic year. Peoria public schools administer *Iowa Tests of Basic Skills* yearly in early October for students in all grades in Title I primary schools, and for students in grades one and three in the district's other primary schools. Holmes restricted the cohort groups to students for whom the district had yearly scores, thus limiting the cohorts to students who were attending Title I schools. Four years of scores exist for Cohort Group 1 ($n = 20$), three for Cohort Group 2 ($n = 26$), two for Cohort Group 3 ($n = 27$), and one for the 1997–98 Valeska Hinton first grade students in Cohort Group 4 ($n = 58$). The number of students in each cohort group having been identified, Holmes then randomly selected matching numbers of students at the same grades from another Title I primary school in the district.

Identical cohort group data analysis procedures were followed for the subtests of *Reading, Vocabulary, Language, Math,* and the *Basic Composite* scores. An alpha level of .05 was used for all statistical tests. These procedures included a mixed-design ANOVA to test for interaction, followed by *t* tests, and a one-way ANOVA to test for simple effects for each cohort. Holmes found no significant differences in growth between Valeska Hinton Center students and control group students, although growth did occur for students in all groups.

READING SCORES

Curious about whether grade-level data analysis would provide similar results, Holmes compared scores across years at the same grade level for the Hinton Center students and the control group students. Figure A.2 presents results of the grade-level analysis of the *Reading* Grade Equivalent Mean Scores for grade one for Cohort Groups 1–4, and Grade 2 for Cohort Groups 1–3.

In the figure, different shadings subdivide the cohort students into two groups: Valeska Hinton Center students when the program was in its first or second year (early in implementation), and Valeska Hinton Center when the program was in its third or fourth year (later in implementation). *Reading* scores for Valeska Hinton Center first graders during the program's third or fourth year of implementation are significantly higher than the scores for first graders during the program's first two years of implementation. Scores for the control group, however, remain essentially flat at Grade 1. The patterns of significance existed for the three other subtests

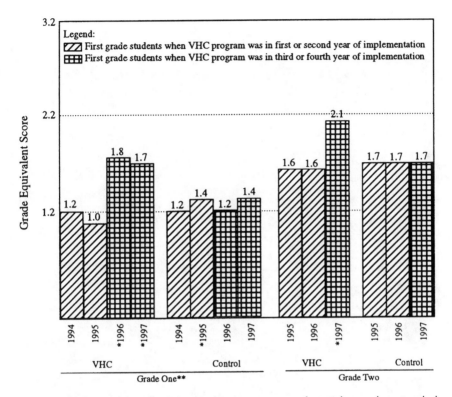

Figure A.2. ITBS reading grade equivalent mean scores for students who attended first grade at Valeska Hinton Center compared with similar students who attended a control school. The Valeska Hinton Center (VHC) students attended the Valeska Hinton Center in preschool and grade one, but attended other Peoria District 150 schools in grade two. Asterisk indicates statistically significant year or group differences (.05 level); double asterisk indicates statistically significant group by year interaction (.01 level).

(*Vocabulary, Language,* and *Math*) and the *Composite* as well. Similar patterns exist for the Grade 2 scores, except that only three cohorts exist at the Grade 2 level, and only one of these (1997) represents students who were in first grade later in the program's implementation.

References

Abbott, J. (1997, March). To be intelligent. *Educational Leadership, 54*(6), 6–10.

Allen, J. (1994, July 6–29). Prudential Cullinan Spring Grove "Southtown housing." *Traveler Weekly,* p. 1.

Alvy, H. B., & Robbins, P. (1998). *If I only knew . . . success strategies for navigating the principalship.* Thousand Oaks, CA: Corwin Press.

Annatucci, J. S. (1996, January). Placing care in the human life cycle. *Journal for a Just and Caring Education, 2*(1), 25–41.

Apple, M. W. (1996). *Cultural politics and education.* New York: Teachers College Press.

Bailey, M. (1989, April 23). Illiteracy loses turf in the projects. *Peoria Journal Star,* pp. A1, A14.

Barth, R. S. (1990). *Improving schools from within.* San Francisco: Jossey-Bass.

Beck, L. G. (1994a). Cultivating a caring school community: One principal's story. In J. Murphy & K. S. Louis (Eds.), *Reshaping the principalship* (pp. 177–202). Thousand Oaks, CA: Corwin Press.

Beck, L. G. (1994b). *Reclaiming educational administration as a caring profession.* New York: Teachers College Press.

Beck, L. G., & Murphy, J. (1993). *Understanding the principalship.* New York: Teachers College Press.

Beck, L. G., & Newman, R. L. (1996). Caring in one urban high school: Thoughts on the interplay among race, class, and gender. In D. Eaker-Rich & J. A. Van Galen (Eds.), *Caring in an unjust world* (pp. 171–198). Albany: State University of New York Press.

Bellah, R. N., Madsen, R., Sullivan, W. M., Swidler, A., & Tipton, S. M. (1985). *Habits of the heart.* New York: Harper & Row.

Bellah, R. N., Madsen, R., Sullivan, W. M., Swidler, A., & Tipton, S. M. (1991). *The good society.* New York: Vintage Books.

Blount, J. M. (1996). Caring and the open moment in educational leadership: A historical perspective. In D. Eaker-Rich & J. A. Van Galen (Eds.), *Caring in an unjust world* (pp. 13–29). Albany: State University of New York Press.

Bogdan, R. C., & Biklen, S. K. (1982). *Qualitative research for education.* Boston: Allyn and Bacon.

Bolman, L. G., & Deal, T. E. (1995). *Leading with soul.* San Francisco: Jossey-Bass.

Bolman, L. G., & Deal, T. E. (1997). *Reframing organizations*. San Francisco: Jossey-Bass.

Brooks, J. G., & Brooks, M. G. (1993). *The case for constructivist classrooms*. Alexandria, VA: Association for Supervision and Curriculum Development.

Brown, D. R. (1998a, July 2). District 150 hires new assistant superintendent. *Peoria Journal Star*, pp. A1, A11.

Brown, D. R. (1998b, August 9). New faces lead Peoria schools. *Peoria Journal Star*, pp. A1, A18.

Caine, R. N., & Caine, G. (1991). *Making connections: Teaching and the human brain*. Alexandria, VA: Association for Supervision and Curriculum Development.

Caine, R. N., & Caine, G. (1997). *Education on the edge of possibility*. Alexandria, VA: Association for Supervision and Curriculum Development.

Center for Prevention Research and Development. (1997). *Valeska Hinton Center Technical Evaluation Report*. Urbana: University of Illinois.

Coffey, A., & Atkinson, P. (1996). *Making sense of qualitative data*. Thousand Oaks, CA: SAGE.

Comer, J. P., Haynes, N. M., Joyner, E. T., & Ben-Avie, M. (1996). *Rallying the whole village*. New York: Teachers College Press.

Courtney, M., & Noblit, G. W. (1994). The principal as caregiver. In A. R. Prillaman, D. J. Eaker, & D. M. Kendrick (Eds.), *The tapestry of caring* (pp. 67–88). Norwood, NJ: Ablex.

Crowson, R. L. (1994). Schools/communities: Strengthening the ties. *Synthesis, 4*(1), 1–6.

Curcio, J. L., & First, P. F. (1995, January). An introduction to the journal for a just and caring education. *Journal for a Just and Caring Education, 1*(1), 3–4.

Damasio, A. R. (1994). *Descartes' error*. New York: Avon.

Dancey, C. J. (1963, August 8). The summing up: World isn't white—or black. *Peoria Journal Star*, pp. A1, A4.

Davies, D. (1991, January). Schools reaching out. *Phi Delta Kappan, 72*(5), 376–382.

Dellar, G. B. (1997, April). *Assessing school climate and its relationship to school improvement*. Paper presented at the Annual Meeting of the American Educational Research Association, Chicago, IL.

Dillard, A. (1974). *Pilgrim at tinker creek*. New York: Harper & Row.

Dillard, C. B. (1995, November). Leading with her life: An African American feminist (re)interpretation of leadership for an urban high school principal. *Educational Administration Quarterly, 31*(4), 539–563.

Drath, W. H., & Palus, C. J. (1994). *Making common sense: Leadership as meaning-making in a community of practice*. Greensboro, NC: Center for Creative Leadership.

Eaker-Rich, D., & Van Galen, J. A. (Eds.). (1996). *Caring in an unjust world*. Albany: State University of New York Press.

Eaker-Rich, D., Van Galen, J. A., & Timothy, E. L. (1996). Conclusion. In D. Eaker-Rich & J. Van Galen (Eds.), *Caring in an unjust world* (pp. 231–242). Albany: State University of New York Press.

Eisner, E. W. (1991). *The enlightened eye*. New York: Macmillan.

Elias, M. J., Zins, J. E., Weissberg, R. P., Frey, K. S., Greenberg, M. T., Haynes, N. M., Kessler, R., Schwab-Stone, M. E., & Shriver, T. P. (1997). *Promoting social and emotional learning.* Alexandria, VA: Association for Supervision and Curriculum Development.

Enomoto, E. K. (1997, August). Negotiating the ethics of care and justice. *Educational Administration Quarterly, 33*(3), 351–370.

Epstein, J. L. (1995, May). School/family/community partnerships. *Phi Delta Kappan, 76*(9), 701–712.

Fisher, B., & Tronto, J. (1990). Toward a feminist theory of caring. In E. K. Abel & M. K. Nelson (Eds.), *Circles of care* (pp. 35–62). Albany: State University of New York Press.

Freire, P. (1992). *Pedagogy of the oppressed* (rev. ed.). New York: Continuum. (Original work published 1970)

Fullan, M. (1997). Emotion and hope: Constructive concepts for complex times. In A. Hargreaves (Ed.), *Rethinking educational change with heart and mind* (pp. 216–233). Alexandria, VA: Association for Supervision and Curriculum Development.

Garrett, R. B. (1973). *The Negro in Peoria.* Unpublished manuscript, Special Collections Center, Bradley University Library.

Gilligan, C. (1982). *In a different voice: Psychological theory and women's development.* Cambridge, MA: Harvard University Press.

Glaser, B. G., & Strauss, A. L. (1967). *The discovery of grounded theory.* Chicago: Aldine.

Greenspan, S. I. (1997). *The growth of the mind.* Reading, MA: Addison-Wesley.

Haberman, M. (1995). *Star teachers of children in poverty.* West Lafayette, IN: Kappa Delta Pi.

Hart, A. W., & Bredeson, P. V. (1996). *The principalship.* New York: McGraw-Hill.

Heifetz, R. A. (1994). *Leadership without easy answers.* Cambridge, MA: Harvard University Press.

Helm, J. H. (1993a). *History of the project.* Unpublished manuscript.

Helm, J. H. (1993b, November). Valeska Hinton early childhood center community collaboration. *Beckley-Cardy Quarterly, 6*(4), 57–59.

Helm, J. H., & Beneke, S. (Eds.). (1996). *Pre-primary curriculum.* Available from Peoria Public Schools, 3202 North Wisconsin Ave., Peoria, IL 61603.

Helm, J. H., Beneke, S., & Steinheimer, K. (1998). *Windows on learning: Documenting young children's work.* New York: Teachers College Press.

Hinton a kids-first appointment. (1998, July 6). *Peoria Journal Star,* p. A4.

Hopkins, E. (1985, March 6). Southtown OK'd under fire. *Peoria Journal Star,* p. A7.

Howard, C. (1992, November 29). School's principal says goodbye to "beloved children." *Peoria Journal Star,* p. B7.

Howard, C. (1993, June 21). District has new center of attention. *Peoria Journal Star,* p. A3.

Hoy, W. K., Tarter, C. J., & Kottkamp, R. B. (1991). *Open schools/healthy schools.* Newbury Park, CA: Sage.

Jensen, E. (1998). *Teaching with the brain in mind*. Alexandria, VA: Association for Supervision and Curriculum Development.

JFK's executive order & Peoria. (1962, November 29). *Peoria Journal Star*, p. A6.

Katz, L. G., & Chard, S. C. (1993). *Engaging children's minds: The project approach*. Norwood, NJ: Ablex.

Killen, M. (1996, January). Justice and care: Dichotomies or coexistence? *Journal for a Just and Caring Education, 2*(1), 42–58.

Klein, J. (1985). *Peoria!*. Peoria, IL: Visual Communications.

Kohn, A. (1991, March). Caring kids. *Phi Delta Kappan, 72*(7), 496–506.

Kohn, A. (1996). *Beyond discipline: From compliance to community*. Alexandria, VA: Association for Supervision and Curriculum Development.

Kolb, D. A., Rubin, E. M., & McIntyre, J. M. (1984). *Organizational psychology: An experiential approach* (4th ed.). Englewood Cliffs, NJ: Prentice Hall.

Kozol, J. (1991). *Savage inequalities*. New York: Crown.

Kozol, J. (1995). *Amazing grace*. New York: Crown.

Kratzer, C. C. (1996, April). *Beyond "effective schools research": Cultivating a caring community in an urban school*. Paper presented at the Annual Meeting of the American Educational Research Association, New York, NY.

Lawrence-Lightfoot, S. (1983). *The good high school*. New York: Basic Books.

Lawrence-Lightfoot, S. (1994). *I've known rivers: Lives of loss and liberation*. New York: Penguin.

Lawrence-Lightfoot, S., & Davis, J. H. (1997). *The art and science of portraiture*. San Francisco: Jossey-Bass.

LeDoux, J. (1996). *The emotional brain*. New York: Simon & Schuster.

Leithwood, K., & Steinbach, R. (1995). *Expert problem solving*. Albany: State University of New York Press.

Lewis, C. C., Schaps, E., & Watson, M. (1995, March). Beyond the pendulum: Creating challenging and caring schools. *Phi Delta Kappan, 76*(7), 547–554.

Lincoln, Y. S., & Guba, E. G. (1985). *Naturalistic inquiry*. Newbury Park, CA: Sage.

Lipsitz, J. (1995, May). Prologue: Why we should care about caring. *Phi Delta Kappan, 76*(9), 665–666.

McLeod, W. T. (Ed.). (1987). *The new Collins dictionary and thesaurus*. London & Glasgow: Collins.

McPherson, R. B., & Crowson, R. L. (1994). The principal as mini-superintendent under Chicago school reform. In J. Murphy & K. S. Louis (Eds.), *Reshaping the principalship* (pp. 57–76). Thousand Oaks, CA: Corwin.

Marshall, C., Patterson, J. A., Rogers, D. L., & Steele, J. R. (1996, April). Caring as career: An alternative perspective for educational administration. *Educational Administration Quarterly, 32*(2), 271–294.

Mayeroff, M. (1971). *On caring*. New York: Harper & Row.

Meisels, S. J., Jablon, J. R., Marsden, D. B., Dichtelmiller, M. L., Dorfman, A. B., & Steele, D. M. (1994). *An overview: The work sampling system*. Ann Arbor, MI: Rebus Planning Associates.

Merriam, S. B. (1988). *Case study research in education*. San Francisco: Jossey-Bass.

Montez, C. (1996). *A Peoria public school: Our story.* Available from the Valeska Hinton Early Childhood Education Center, 800 West Romeo B. Garrett Avenue, Peoria, IL 61605.

Near South Side general neighborhood renewal plan. (1967, October). Southfield, MI: Vilican-Lehman & Associates, Inc.

Newburg, N. A. (1995, May). Clusters: Organizational patterns for caring. *Phi Delta Kappan, 76*(9), 713–717.

Noblit, G. W. (1993a). Power and caring. *American Educational Research Journal, 30*(1), 23–38.

Noblit, G. W. (1993b, April). *Instituting caring in a school: Principal contradictions.* Paper presented at the Annual Meeting of the American Educational Research Association, Atlanta, GA.

Noddings, N. (1984). *Caring: A feminine approach to ethics and moral education.* Berkeley: University of California Press.

Noddings, N. (1992). *The challenge to care in schools.* New York: Teachers College Press.

Noddings, N. (1995, May). Teaching themes of care. *Phi Delta Kappan, 76*(9), 675–679.

Pugh, T. (1963a, July 31). 6 "mixed" neighborhoods here and no 2 alike. *Peoria Journal Star,* pp. A1, A4.

Pugh, T. (1963b, August 1). Whites replacing Negroes in many areas. *Peoria Journal Star,* pp. A1, A2.

Quint, S. (1994). *Schooling homeless children.* New York: Teachers College Press.

Reeves, M. (1995, October 26). *Parent Advisory Board meeting minutes.* Available from Valeska Hinton Early Childhood Education Center, 800 West Romeo B. Garrett Avenue, Peoria, IL 61605.

Roethke, T. (1961). *Words for the wind.* Bloomington, IN: Indiana University Press.

Rossi, R. K., & Stringfield, S. C. (1995, September). What we must do for students placed at risk. *Phi Delta Kappan, 77*(1), 73–76.

Ryan, S., & Friedlaender, D. (1996, April). *Becoming caring: Changing relationships to create responsive schools.* Paper presented at the Annual Meeting of the American Educational Research Association, New York, NY.

Sams, J. (1993). *The 13 original clan mothers.* San Francisco: HarperCollins.

Seidman, I. E. (1991). *Interviewing as qualitative research.* New York: Teachers College Press.

Sergiovanni, T. J. (1991). *The principalship* (2nd ed.). Boston: Allyn and Bacon.

Sergiovanni, T. J. (1994). *Building community in schools.* San Francisco: Jossey-Bass.

Sergiovanni, T. J. (1996). *Leadership for the schoolhouse.* San Francisco: Jossey-Bass.

Shakeshaft, C. (1987). *Women in educational administration.* Newbury Park, CA: Sage.

Sneve, V. D. H. (1986). Women of the circle. In H. F. Thompson, A. R. Huseboe, & S. O. Looney (Eds.), *A common land, a diverse people* (pp. 130–147). Freeman, SD: Pine Hill Press.

Starratt, R. J. (1991, May). Building an ethical school: A theory for practice in educational leadership. *Educational Administration Quarterly, 27*(2), 185–202.

Starratt, R. J. (1996). *Transforming educational administration: Meaning, community, and excellence.* New York: McGraw Hill.

Sylwester, R. (1995). *A celebration of neurons: An educator's guide to the human brain.* Alexandria, VA: Association for Supervision and Curriculum Development.

Sylwester, R. (1997, March). On using knowledge about our brain. *Educational Leadership, 54*(6), 16–19.

Task Force on Education of Young Adolescents. (1989). *Turning points: Preparing American youth for the 21st century.* New York: Carnegie Council on Adolescent Development.

Ubben, G. C., & Hughes, L. W. (1997). *The principal.* Boston: Allyn and Bacon.

Valeska Hinton Early Childhood Education Center Parent Handbook. (1998). Available from the Valeska Hinton Early Childhood Education Center, 800 West Romeo B. Garrett Avenue, Peoria, IL 61605.

Valeska Hinton's legacy. (1991, September 25). *Peoria Journal Star,* p. A4.

Ward, C. E. (1996). *Recultivating Froebel's kindergarten for a post-modern society.* Unpublished doctoral dissertation, Southern Illinois University, Carbondale.

Williams, B., & Newcombe, E. (1994). Building on the strengths of urban learners. *Educational Leadership, 52*(6), 75–78.

Wolcott, H. F. (1990). *Writing up qualitative research.* Newbury Park, CA: Sage.

Index

About the Author

Having earned a Ph.D. in Administration, Curriculum, and Instruction from the University of Nebraska–Lincoln in 1990, Linda L. Lyman was a faculty member in the Department of Educational Leadership and Human Development at Bradley University in Peoria, Illinois, during 1990–99. She coordinated the Leadership in Educational Administration master's-level principalship program. Dr. Lyman's academic credentials include a B.A. in English from Northwestern University and a Master of Arts in Teaching from Harvard University. Before becoming a professor, she held a variety of professional positions in education at the local, regional, and state levels. In the fall of 1999, Dr. Lyman joined the Department of Educational Administration and Foundations at Illinois State University as an Associate Professor.